like a
boy
but not
a boy

like a boy but not a boy

Navigating Life, Mental Health, and Parenthood outside the Gender Binary

andrea bennett

ARSENAL PULP PRESS
VANCOUVER

LIKE A BOY BUT NOT A BOY
Copyright © 2020 by andrea bennett

SECOND PRINTING: 2022

ARSENAL PULP PRESS
Suite 202 – 211 East Georgia St.
Vancouver, BC V6A 1Z6
Canada
arsenalpulp.com

The publisher gratefully acknowledges the support of the Canada Council for the Arts and the British Columbia Arts Council for its publishing program, and the Government of Canada, and the Government of British Columbia (through the Book Publishing Tax Credit Program), for its publishing activities.

Arsenal Pulp Press acknowledges the xʷməθkʷəy̓əm (Musqueam), Sḵwx̱wú7mesh (Squamish), and səl̓ilwətaʔɬ (Tsleil-Waututh) Nations, custodians of the traditional, ancestral, and unceded territories where our office is located. We pay respect to their histories, traditions, and continuous living cultures and commit to accountability, respectful relations, and friendship.

"Like a Boy but Not a Boy" was included in the anthology *Swelling with Pride*, edited by Sara Graefe (Halfmoon Bay, BC: Caitlin Press, 2018); "Mom, Dad, Other" was published as "I'm a Non-Binary Parent. There Still Isn't Space for Me," *Xtra*, May 10, 2019; "On Class and Writing" was published as "The Year in Work," *Hazlitt*, December 9, 2015; and "Tomboy" was published as "The In-Between Space," *Hazlitt*, September 18, 2018.

Gwendolyn MacEwen's "Certain Flowers" copyright © to the estate of Gwendolyn MacEwen. Permission to reprint lines from this poem provided by David MacKinnon, executor for the estate of Gwendolyn MacEwen.

Cover and text design by Jazmin Welch
Edited by Shirarose Wilensky
Proofread by Alison Strobel

Printed and bound in Canada

Library and Archives Canada Cataloguing in Publication:
Title: Like a boy but not a boy : navigating life, mental health, and parenthood outside the gender binary / andrea bennett.
Names: Bennett, Andrea (Andrea Kathleen), author.
Identifiers: Canadiana (print) 20200211609 | Canadiana (ebook) 20200211692 | ISBN 9781551528212 (softcover) | ISBN 9781551528229 (HTML)
Subjects: LCSH: Bennett, Andrea (Andrea Kathleen) | LCSH: Gender-nonconforming people. | LCSH: Gender identity. | LCSH: Gender nonconformity. | LCSH: Gender-nonconforming people—Mental health. | LCSH: Sexual minority parents. | LCSH: Parenthood. | LCGFT: Essays.
Classification: LCC HQ18.55 .B46 2020 | DDC 305.3—dc23

CONTENTS

INTRODUCTION

LIKE A BOY BUT NOT A BOY is a book that I began writing on the bus and SkyTrain between Surrey and Vancouver, British Columbia. My first notes were mostly about the process of returning to work in an office after having a baby, and then leaving that baby at home with my partner. At the time, we were referring to ourselves as the milk parent and the beard parent; my role was to provide the milk, and between working, commuting, and pumping, I was exhausted. My favourite SkyTrain seat—one I often managed to snag because I boarded at the terminus station—was at the very rear of the train, facing backward, with more than enough legroom and space to spread out and write in my notebook or work on my laptop. All the new essays in the book owe their initial pacing to the SkyTrain.

Like a Boy but Not a Boy contains thirteen more or less personal essays, covering a range of topics from queer pregnancy and parenting to nonbinary identity, bike mechanics, mortality, anxiety, class, and mental illness.

It also contains a sixteen-part essay titled "Everyone Is Sober and No One Can Drive," which is drawn from interviews with queer millennials who grew up in small communities across Canada. My intention with "Everyone Is Sober" is to give snapshots of what it was like to come of age right around the time that same-sex marriage was legalized in this country —a cultural crux point that may be looked back on as a definitive marker between "before" and "after" but that is perhaps better seen as one red push-pin on a transitional arc. The segments resulting from these inter-views are listed by the subjects' first names ("Jane" is a pseudonym) in the table of contents and seeded throughout the book.

Like a Boy but Not a Boy is ultimately about the simultaneously banal but engrossing task of living in a body. Although most of the essays are about living in my body, I'm very grateful to the sixteen other queer millen-nials who shared their stories so that we might become a type of chorus.

1

TOMBOY

IN GRADE FOUR, OUR CLASS WAS IN A PORTABLE about 100 metres beyond the school's back door. A small wooden porch flanked by two railings and a set of stairs led up to the portable; it also provided a multi-level platform useful for playing WWF WrestleMania. One other girl sometimes played with us, but mostly it was just me and a whole bunch of boys. The goal was to hurl ourselves at each other hard enough to pin—to push and jostle and launch off the porch onto an unsuspecting crowd of wrestlers. The boys weren't my friends, but they let me play with them. (Sports is all about numbers.) I had long hair, but it was unkempt, and this was the era of nineties Jaromír Jágr—his glorious, curly mullet unfurling from his hockey helmet in much the same way my dark waves bunched at my shoulders.

That year, I turned nine and was finally allowed to play hockey. The first time I knocked over a fellow girl—not on my team—I stopped skating and helped her back to her feet as my father hollered from the stands. Afterwards, he and my coaches told me to "use my size," the way it was beneficial on the porch behind the portable.

That year, in school, we played a math game called Around the World, based on the times tables, in which the goal was to circle the classroom, defeating your classmates one by one. That year, drunk on wrestling and hockey and math—a subject I understood to be best suited to real (read: male) nerds—I requested that my classmates call me Andy. They did not comply.

I grew up in a time and place—born in 1984, raised in a small town called Dundas, Ontario—when gender roles were binary. I grew up in a place where my favourite tomboy classmate later ridiculed my unshaven legs. I grew up in a place where, when I was walking to work or the library, people yelled gendered, homophobic slurs out of their cars. I grew up with a mother I thoroughly confused and disappointed, just by virtue of being myself. It's hard to say what kind of a person I'd be today if these conditions had been different. Given these conditions, though, I took refuge in the word "tomboy."

THE WORD "TOMBOY" FIRST EMERGED in the mid-sixteenth century to describe rude, forward boys. A couple decades later, it began to apply to women—more specifically, bold and immodest, impudent and unchaste women. Soon after that, the term found the home we're familiar with, referring to girls who behaved like "spirited or boisterous" boys. (Men got to keep "tomcat"—creepy if you've ever googled "cat sex" after hearing alleyway yowling in the middle of the night.)

By the time I hit elementary school, tomboy's denotation had remained unchanged, but its connotation had shifted: acting like a spirited and bois- terous boy wasn't such a bad thing. Second-wave feminism had crested, power suits had come and gone, and we all understood that embodying certain aspects of masculinity provided a shortcut—albeit tenuous—to power in adulthood, and freedom in childhood. As Jack Halberstam writes in his 1998 book *Female Masculinity*, tomboyism tended, at that time, to be "associated with a 'natural' desire for the greater freedom and mobility enjoyed by boys." Of course, there were boundaries: eschewing girls' clothing altogether, say, or asking your classmates to opt for a more masculine version of your name.

"Tomboy," as an adult term, is most often applied to straight women who are somewhat masculine or boyish, or maybe "androgynous"—a word most often applied by the mainstream to masculine women with model-like proportions, proportions that are clothing-flexible because they are narrow and boxy. The first sentence of Lizzie Garrett Mettler's introduction to *Tomboy Style: Beyond the Boundaries of Fashion*, goes like so: "When I arrived on campus for my first day at Brooks School in North Andover, Massachusetts, I was thirteen and as plumb a tomboy as any." A couple of paragraphs later, when Mettler describes breaking her collarbone playing field hockey, she writes that her new Brooks best friend, Kingsley Woolworth, "decorated [her] sling with Lilly Pulitzer fabric sourced from a pair of my mother's cigarette pants." Mettler's tom- boyhood fashion icons, featured in the full-colour book, are universally thin, generally white, and cover the usual gamut from Coco Chanel to Patti Smith, Carolyn Bessette-Kennedy, and Diane Keaton, with more contemporary additions like Tilda Swinton and Janelle Monáe.

My favourite photo is probably the one of Eartha Kitt, in mid-swing, playing baseball. Most of the other photos and icons—not to take anything away from these great women—don't include people like me. I don't and can't see myself in these wealthy celebrities: their small breasts, their bony shoulders, the ease with which a pair of trousers glides over their hips and thighs. Taken together with Mettler's narrative, these images frame "tomboy" as a way of being a woman that fits quite neatly into what we expect of "woman": a conventional BMI, tousled hair, a camera-friendly approach. Bodies with hips cocked, odalisque'd across the hood of a fifties car. Style from brands and stories that are very parochially New York, or what you'd call continental, European. Style that reaches out to rich women who want to marry rich men, style that lets them know everything will be okay: here is a way forward that will still appeal to the men and women in your social niche.

SEVERAL YEARS AGO, I WAS EATING LUNCH AT A CAFÉ in Greenpoint, Brooklyn. Behind me, a mom and daughter spoke Polish while they waited for their order. They were a matched set: both blonde and blue-eyed, similar facial structure, similar feminine clothing styles, similar body types.

When I was very young and could be forced into puffy-sleeved dresses, could be convinced or strong-armed into wearing curls and tights, my mother foresaw a future where we would be a set. My hair wasn't blonde like hers, my eyes weren't blue, my ears stuck out farther from my head than they were supposed to, but none of these things was immutable.

At eight or nine I began to grow. My body shot up and broadened. My legs lengthened, my belly got round, I became chubby, grew breasts. Next to my peers, who still looked like children, I felt monstrous. My mom urged the hairdresser to "soften" my face with feathered bangs. We fought about clothes. I wanted to dress like the boy from two doors down who wore low-riding shorts and untucked T-shirts; wearing my pants like that, my mom said, would draw attention to my stomach. We bought clothing in aspirational sizes. We put me on a diet. I starved and binged. I forgot to close my legs when I was made to wear a skirt. Instead of being part of a set with my mom, I resented her as much as I resented my inability to give her what she wanted from me.

The word "tomboy" provided me with my first out. Being a tomboy offered me a way to pursue masculinity from what felt like a failed female body. I gave up mimicking girlhood, accepted a ruptured relationship with my mother, and slowly began to build a relationship with my body and my selfhood that wasn't based in self-negation. The world I grew up in—the world we live in now—still places an inordinate amount of pressure on female bodies to be consumable; opting out of femininity, even privately, freed me to see myself as a whole person, and it also freed me to interrogate the legitimacy of the boundaries I was breaching with my monstrosity. Tomboyhood offered me a kind of self-acceptance I never got to experience as a girl.

But conventional gender-code breaking—allowed, within boundaries, for girls—ends, too often, with adulthood. As Halberstam writes, "If adolescence for boys represents a rite of passage ... for girls, adolescence is a lesson in restraint, punishment, and repression." In popular culture (Pippi Longstocking, for example), tomboyism is often folded into narratives about resisting adulthood; there's a tacit understanding that with time, a tomboy will grow out of her (his, their) affinity for masculine presentation, masculine-coded pastimes, masculine-coded work. And so "tomboy" gets roped in, like everything else, to safety and convention—swanning into simple, elegant, usually white, womanhood. A conventionally attractive woman devouring a burger in a men's magazine profile, an unadorned silk dress.

My masculinity never turned men's mag icon. I have never been an uncomplicated body in a silky dress; instead, I began to identify with the world of female masculinity best understood and embraced by queer theory. I pursued masculine-coded work, becoming a bike mechanic. I grew up and, though I dated men, came to identify as queer.

For more than a year, I have had a *BuzzFeed* video bookmarked on my computer: "What Is Female Masculinity?" I watch it about once a month. The video starts with identifications: "I don't really identify with anything, but if anything, I guess it would be butch"; "MOC, which is, like, masculine of centre"; "genderqueer butch mahoo"; two "gender-neutral"s; "LHB: long-haired butch." Everybody has similar but diverging things to say about masculinity, female masculinity, aesthetics, and the benefits and disadvantages of being female and masculine in a world that prizes many aspects of masculinity. Near the end, one of the participants says, "A lot of times, butch women are blessed with the burden of boobs. That's a very funny cross to bear on top of everything else."

I have large breasts—boobs—and like many people who experience gender dysphoria, I do everything in my power to keep this detail from the general public (I own a binder, surreptitiously wear sports bras under collared shirts, curve my wide shoulders forward in an attempt to hide myself). Often, I'm proud of myself and I accept my body. But sometimes, I feel alone, quite alone. I can't sum up the power of watching someone express my secret shame as a warmly funny in-joke.

I understand why people balk at labels—why further subdivide the world? But I think of them—tomboy, butch, genderqueer, MOC—as functional and hopeful. If I can't describe who I am in this world—I am who I am, whether or not I can describe it—then I can't seek out others like me.

IN 2016, MEREDITH HALE, CREATOR OF THE MOMMY A TO Z BLOG, wrote "Don't Call My Daughter a Tomboy" for the *Huffington Post*. Hale's daughter comes home from school one day and announces that she feels she is like a boy—in fact, a tomboy—because she likes sports. Hale writes, in part, that she herself had once "been guilty of using the label 'tomboy'"— but only before she "knew better." The previous year, feminist Catherine Connors wrote a piece on *Her Bad Mother* (later reprinted by *Medium* and BUST) called "Don't Call Her a Tomboy." Connors's kid, who rides dirt bikes, self-identifies as a tomboy. "I wouldn't call you a tomboy, sweetie. I think that you're you," Connors tells her kid. "And you like a lot of different things, and they're not just 'boy things' or 'girl things,' they're things that you like." Similarly, Hale wants her daughter to grow up embracing her femininity and at the same time feeling free to pursue whatever sports and pastimes draw her attention.

Eventually, Connors comes to the conclusion that these ongoing conversations are not really about tomboys, after all—they are about feminism. That girls and boys can contain multitudes. That gender stereotypes must be challenged. That parents must contest the ways in which society —with its pink aisles and camo prints—boxes in boys and girls.

Has our conception of gender changed so much that the in-between space that was so useful for me as a child—that is useful for me as an adult—is no longer necessary? After mulling over these pieces—and, more broadly, the differences between mainstream feminism and queer feminism—I wish there was room to embrace both "tomboy" and the fight to move beyond gender stereotyping. I wonder: How would I have felt if I received these messages from my mother? What if, instead, we told kids that girls and boys can do and like and be who they want—but if they're not a girl, or not a boy, that's okay, too?

I have done a lot of work to disentangle myself from misogyny—to embrace what exists of my own femininity, to move past the ways I rejected femininity broadly because it was foisted upon me. I can't help but feel that mainstream feminism has not done the same amount of work to understand genderqueerness, to understand trans identities. Why, otherwise, would you call to kill a term that still holds some usefulness for me, and others like me? If the world has told us for much of our lives that we are not quite women, and, moreover, the labels "girl" and "woman" never quite fit, is it our responsibility to forcibly expand girlhood and womanhood until it grudgingly accepts us? Can I not just be woman-adjacent in peace?

Identity exists at the crux point of internal and external pressures—who we feel we are, and how others see us. Far from being discrete, one feeds into the other. I have no way of knowing how I'd feel if I hadn't spent my youth feeling shamed into, and failing at, femininity. I wouldn't be a feminine woman; maybe I'd feel more comfortable stretching "woman" until it fit, but also, maybe not. As it stands, I'm not a woman, and I'm not a man; I'm not a tomboy anymore, either, though kernels of tomboyhood remain useful for me. In adolescence, tomboyhood offered me a positive way to describe myself instead of repeating "I'm not, I'm not, I'm not." It emphasized doing rather than being; it offered the option of finding power, and community, and freedom, in monstrosity.

david

DAVID IS THIRTY-FIVE, QUEER, AND MOSTLY CIS. He sometimes feels a little non-gender-y, but not in a very defined way. Usually like, "What would aliens think about our construct of gender?" David doesn't really even care enough to pick a label. If he had to, he'd choose agender.

David was born in Ontario, but because his dad was in the army, his family moved to Germany a month or two after he was born. David lived on an English-speaking military base in Germany until he was five. Then his family moved to Saint-Hubert, just outside Montreal. They were there until David was eight. Finally, they moved to Fredericton, New Brunswick, where David lived until he was seventeen. He went to school in English in Germany, in French in Saint-Hubert, and in English in Fredericton.

All of David's earliest memories are of Germany and of travelling around Europe. He doesn't really remember Saint-Hubert, but he thinks it was probably stressful, since he doesn't remember it. He didn't really speak the language.

When his family arrived in Fredericton, David didn't know that was where he'd be until he left home to go to university. The one nice thing about moving there was that his family lived with civilians in a regular neighbourhood for the first time. Living on base, only with other military people, had sometimes felt a bit like living in a cult. They moved to the suburban neighbourhood of New Maryland, about a ten-minute drive from Fredericton, and bought a nice house, on about an acre of land, right next to a forest. The edge of their property ended at the forest line, and David spent a lot of time in the woods.

David doesn't remember when he actually realized that being queer was a thing. At fourteen, he watched Jack on *Dawson's Creek* come out. That was when he realized that coming out was something he'd have to do. He came out to his friend Maggie first, at fifteen. His parents learned soon after. The closest he got to telling them was a moment when he was sitting on the living room floor watching TV with them, but he didn't do it. And then he was really angsty, so his mom read his journal. And that's how she found out. David's mom told his dad, and his dad had a very uneventful conversation with him about it. Like, "So your mother tells me you're gay." "Mm-hmm." "And that you didn't clean out the litter box."

David has an older sister. They were close until puberty, but she grew up first and was out exploring, away from David, so they grew apart a little. They're close again now. David wasn't very close to either of his parents as a teenager. Now, his relationship is good with his dad, and not good with his mom. David feels like his dad is more open to growing and changing and acknowledging the impact that he's had on him. He's made some remarks that have felt apologetic to David, whereas his mom has never really been interested in acknowledging any effect that she's had on him.

David was at his sister's cottage once, and his stepmom asked if she could take a photo. His dad brought David and his sister in close, and David made some comment like, "I thought you taught us to never touch each other." And his dad was like, "Oh yeah, sorry about that." He acknowledged it, and apologized for not expressing physical affection when David was a kid.

For David's master's in social work, he had to write a paper about the intergenerational emotional patterns in his family, which required asking his parents questions. David's dad was very open to sharing information, and he also apologized for going away for a large portion of David's grade twelve year. That year, it was just David and his mom, and they fought all the time.

There were other out kids at David's high school. At least, there were after his mom outed them. In grade eleven, he started hanging out with two gay kids in grade twelve, and he started seeing one of them. They were sort of out to their friends, but not super out. One day, David was supposed to go home, but instead, he hung out with the kids from grade twelve. David's mom found out where the boy lived, went to his house, and told his parents that he was gay. David still doesn't know why, to this day. The boy immediately wanted nothing to do with David.

David's high school principal didn't like him because David handed out a survey about gay attitudes and experiences for his grade twelve sociology class. He handed it out to his friends, some of whom were out in high school and some of whom came out later, but also to other, random students. Someone reported him, and he got called into the principal's office. His sociology teacher didn't stand up for him. His principal yelled at him and said the survey was inappropriate. The principal stood up and walked around his desk so that he was standing over David, his cheeks quivering he was so angry. After, one of his classmates who was an intern at a TV studio got David on a local show to talk about high school homophobia. David badmouthed his principal on TV. It was funny. David was almost prevented from attending prom. Not because he had a gay date, but because he wasn't dressed appropriately. They did eventually let him in. It may have been a power play.

When David was coming of age in Fredericton, the city still felt very homophobic. It was twenty years ago, so that's part of it, but also, New Brunswick tended to have more traditional, Christian values than other places. For the entirety of high school, David was looking forward to leaving. In every teen soap he watched, his favourite season was the one where they went to university. He was really excited to do it himself.

David ended up going to the University of Guelph. It wasn't an easy transition, though. He lived in residence for his first two months and then moved out and got his own apartment. His room in residence was nice, with big bay windows, but it felt like he'd moved in with his high school football team. He needed to get out. He'd signed up for psychology as his major when he applied to university, and it worked out—he liked studying it and was drawn to learning more about himself. The people he met felt like his people, but he was still pretty much just living in his head.

It took until David graduated from university and moved to Toronto for him to really feel comfortable being himself. He felt pretty closed off in Guelph, even though he had queer friends and dated people there. He found a big queer community in Toronto, where everyone was really weird and not like a lot of other queer people he'd met before. He felt a lot of kinship with them. Eventually, he felt more comfortable opening up. It was age, partially, and doing work on himself. He figured out how to be more open.

When David got to Toronto, he lived a carefree life for the first few years. He was a bartender until he was twenty-six or so, partying all the time. David abused alcohol in those years, but then he started dealing with the emotions he'd been avoiding, and moved from bartending back into the structure of school. The consequences of drinking started to outweigh the benefits, and he stopped drinking excessively. He only drinks a bit now and no longer has a problematic relationship with alcohol. There's an intensity to sobriety that can feel like being on drugs. When David stopped drinking excessively, he felt more anxious at first, and then he felt sharper than he'd been in a long time.

He thinks that part of that time of excess in his twenties might be attributable to the fact that queer millennials didn't really get a youth—the freedom to explore that exists for some in their teenage years and early twenties is often devoted to repression, or a focus on escape and survival—so they have had to live it later, once they found their communities. It may also be that being queer is like rewriting a script: when you break one of the main rules, you just aren't as willing to follow other kinds of rules, and you're not as willing to follow traditional life paths.

john

JOHN WAS BORN IN 1991. They're non-binary. They grew up on a pretty big farm, in northwestern Ontario, near Lake of the Woods, with an older brother and a younger brother. It was a very pretty part of Ontario, near the Canadian Shield—so, nice and rocky. Where John grew up, there was sometimes a grocery store. It would change hands every couple of years. There was a church, and there was a school. There were maybe 100 kids in kindergarten through grade eight in the entire school. John's year was relatively large, and it was six people. Their older brother was one of two people in his grade. Many of the people in the area were farmers. John's family raised beef cattle. Growing up meant mostly being stuck on the farm or in school, and occasionally seeing other people.

John's family home was about 2,000 square feet. It had plywood floors that never ended up getting any flooring on top of them. It was a built-for-efficiency house that wasn't very fancy. A bungalow with a crawl space for a basement. The walls were extra thick, because when John's dad built the house he was like, "I need to have as much insulation in this house as possible."

They went to the Canadian school that was just about a kilometre from their farm for kindergarten through grade six, and then they crossed the US border and went to a school in Baudette, Minnesota, for seventh through twelfth grade. Their mom drove them across the border every day to school.

John had to leave home to go to university. Their parents were really pro-education. There wasn't anywhere to go in the area, apart from maybe a community college in Fort Frances an hour and a half away. John's dad really wanted someone to take over the farm, so there was that pressure, but John knew they wouldn't be suited to it. If John wasn't going to take over the farm, there was nothing really for them in their hometown.

John really didn't have much of a concept of queerness until they went to university. They knew gay people existed, but they didn't know anyone who was out. Everything they heard about being gay growing up was pejorative, insults. They didn't have a sense of there being any community.

John's mom is pretty open-minded, and their dad just doesn't care about that sort of thing, for the most part. John is not exactly out with their parents, but their mom follows their Twitter account, so she sees John tweeting about queer themes and topics, and being non-binary. It's probably something they should have a conversation about at some point. But John is not very good at having these kinds of conversations.

As John started learning more about trans people, they remember being really fascinated but not really knowing why. They were maybe a junior in university when they learned being trans was a thing. They didn't learn that being non-binary was a possibility until after they graduated. It wasn't something they encountered until they came across A. Light Zachary, a writer who had they/them pronouns in their Twitter bio, and they were like, "What does *that* mean?" John learned more and thought, *Oh, wow, that's me.*

John gave themselves permission to identify as non-binary a couple years ago, when they were living in Jersey City, New Jersey, after finishing their coursework for grad school. John was working on their thesis and had just broken up with someone. They'd been thinking a lot about gender and decided they needed to give themselves space to figure it out. After a lot of questioning, and a deep depressive period, they came to the conclusion they were non-binary. It was freeing. In part because of its inclusivity. They can say they're non-binary, and it doesn't erase their life before that. They were a boy for a while, and that was fine, but it wasn't working out. For John, the term "non-binary" felt like it acknowledged a connection to their past and made space for the fact that they sometimes don't care if people call them "he."

John now lives in Kansas City, Missouri, which has a population of several hundred thousand people. Very sprawling. Kansas City is very liberal, for the most part, despite the fact that it is in Kansas and also Missouri. If you go to the 'burbs, it gets a little bit more conservative. John doesn't necessarily read as queer from the outside. They paint their nails and wear rings and have long hair. Over the last year they started using "Elizabeth" as their middle name, because a friend used to call them John Elizabeth, and Elizabeth is their mom's middle name. But they still don't come out to that many people in day-to-day life. They have trouble advocating for themselves, so they just accept what's given to them. People say "sir" all the time.

John feels less comfortable whenever they go anywhere outside of Kansas City. Their partner's family is from Oklahoma, so they'll go down to Tulsa and they'll keep their hands in their pockets when they're fuelling up the car in Oklahoma or southern Missouri. Or sometimes they won't paint their nails. It depends on where they're going.

Going back home—that's a different beast. John is the middle kid, and their brothers will kind of tease them. Their little brother can be mean. Seeing both of their brothers together can be bad. One on one, they're fine. But if they're together, it can be a nightmare.

John will paint their nails when they go home, but they've never sat down and explained their gender to their parents. They don't know how much their parents have deduced. Recently, too, a friend of theirs from high school has started saying that they should hang out. John isn't sure about it. They'd want to make sure their friend was aware of their identity beforehand. And maybe the friend wouldn't care, or maybe he would be confused. It feels weird, like this other world trying to collide with their current world.

Whenever John tweets, they think, My mom might see this, because she follows about five people. She's kind of like a mom on Facebook, just responding to everything. John will see her in a conversation with someone like writer Joshua Whitehead and be like, "All right. She's doing her thing. It's okay."

2

LIVING WITH DEATH

IN 1993, WHEN I WAS EIGHT YEARS OLD, the FBI and the Bureau of Alcohol, Tobacco, Firearms, and Explosives stormed Mount Carmel Center ranch. Located just outside Waco, Texas, the ranch was home to David Koresh and his Branch Davidian followers; the group believed that the second coming of Christ was imminent, and they'd begun to stockpile guns and ammunition against the coming chaos. Anthony Storr's *Feet of Clay*, a book about gurus, compares Koresh's "regime" on the ranch to Jonestown, the Guyana enclave where preacher Jim Jones psychologically and physically abused his followers, rationing their food and sleep and coercing more than 900 of them into drinking cyanide-laced Flavor Aid. The siege on Mount Carmel lasted fifty-one days. In late February, after a brutal and fiery standoff that resulted in ten deaths, Koresh allowed a group of children to leave the ranch when the ATF arrived—but kept back at least twenty-five kids, many of whom he'd fathered with women and girls in the group. In mid-April, the FBI and the ATF initiated a final raid on the ranch using the kind of weaponry usually reserved for war. Seventy-six of the eighty-five Branch Davidians left inside the compound died, either by fire—three fires erupted in different areas of the ranch as government agents attempted to penetrate the buildings—or by gunshot wounds from fellow believers.

Koresh, Storr writes, was obsessed with the Book of Revelation. Before he'd joined the Branch Davidians and become a leader within the group, he'd flitted from religion to religion before landing for a while—before he was ousted for harassing the pastor's daughter—in a Seventh-day Adventist congregation. The founders of that church originally believed that Christ's second coming would occur by October 22, 1844—a date based on the prophecy of an influential Baptist preacher called William Miller. After that day came and went, a group of Millerites formed the Seventh-day Adventist Church, so named because they considered the seventh day of the week (and therefore the Sabbath) to be Saturday, and because they believed the apocalypse, though it hadn't occurred exactly as originally predicted, was nonetheless still coming soon.

My memory of watching the Waco siege on TV is very clear; I also remember learning about Jonestown, which was cited as the predecessor, at least spiritually, of many of the end-times cults that crescendoed in the nineties. Less well-known than Waco was the Order of the Solar Temple, a small but geographically dispersed cult active in France, Switzerland, and Canada, which believed that a great "transition" was imminent and Christ would soon come again as a solar god-king. The OST was responsible for a rash of dozens of murders and suicides in 1994 and 1997, all grouped around equinoxes and solstices; founders believed the group was linked to the Knights Templar, and one founder claimed to be the third reincarnation of Jesus Christ. And Heaven's Gate was a group whose beliefs married Christianity with science fiction—that God was an elite extraterrestrial and heaven was a physical place, the next evolutionary step above humanity. Heaven's Gate believed that a UFO, which they would board to participate in the rapture, was to arrive after the passing of the incredibly bright comet Hale–Bopp. To join the UFO, thirty-nine members opted to leave their bodies by suicide in late March 1997—a tactic, they reasoned, that had more or less worked for Jesus.

I remember news clips about the OST, and I remember the laughing disbelief most North Americans had for Heaven's Gate. My first exposure to it wasn't The Simpsons' episode "The Joy of Sect," which aired the year after the suicides—a cult comes to Springfield and promises spaceship transport to the planet Blisstonia—but I remember watching that, too.

PERHAPS IT WAS COMING OF AGE IN THE NINETIES, when much of this was happening—in real time, and then digestible again through documentaries on HBO and A&E—that first sparked my interest in millenarian beliefs. The idea that the end of the world will someday come via the arrival, or re-arrival, of Christ is common to several different belief systems, but the idea that it is coming soon is particular to fewer: Seventh-day Adventists, Mormons, Jehovah's Witnesses, several non-denominational protestant sects, including Endtime Ministries (handle @EndtimeInc), whose Twitter tagline reads, "Preaching the Gospel of the Kingdom to every person on earth ... Because the Endtime is Now!" (The existence of these groups explains, in part, why a segment of the Christian right in North America is so obsessed with Israel—most millenarian-focused

Christian denominations believe that a series of end-times-related events will unfold in Israel before the advent of the rapture, and some groups believe this so fiercely that they are working to *hasten* those events.)

The first thing I remember watching on television as a child was not *Sesame Street* or *The Raccoons* or *Barney & Friends*. It was aerial footage of Mount Carmel burning, reconstructed footage of the Oklahoma City bombings, one-hour specials devoted to murder and embezzlement and hit men narrated by men with deep, gravelly voices, establishing the early norms of the burgeoning genre of true crime.

I stayed up late watching these shows with my father because I could not sleep; I could not sleep because, at the age of seven or eight, I'd begun to wrestle with the existential truth that I would someday die. That my consciousness would be extinguished and I would cease to exist. In the beginning, I stared out the window and let my consciousness float past the ravine I could see from my room, down the paths I knew crept through the conservation area by my house, beyond hills and valleys and towns and cities, and out into the deep, deeply alone space of the universe. When I couldn't take this expansion, or the idea of nothingness, anymore, I went to the basement and watched TV.

Nothing particularly terrible or traumatizing took place in my childhood, at least related to death; I had six living grandparents, never witnessed a serious accident, lived in a suburb that experienced very little violent crime, never had to come to terms, even, with losing a pet. My brother wasn't similarly obsessed, even though our father had given us both the same rational, calm, atheistic explanation of what would happen when we finally breathed our last breaths. But I thought about death and dying several times a day, and the fear culminated when the sun set, before

I ceded my consciousness to sleep—a practice that inevitably felt like a test for a much longer and more permanent cessation.

Looking back, it's possible that I was drawn to true crime because I was seeking an unseekable meaning, or narrative structure, in death. Perhaps I was drawn to end-times beliefs because the fears felt intuitively similar to my own but came ready-made with an idea of what happened after. Or maybe, initially, it was easier than that: I was drawn to watching dramas about dying because I was drawn to explore what terrified me, even if exploring what terrified me worsened the terror. I wanted to live forever; if I couldn't, then I'd explore all the ways people believed things would end.

IN ELEMENTARY SCHOOL, our music teacher had a distinctive grey bob and played the acoustic guitar. She taught us morose songs about the environment (in addition to David Koresh, the world was also obsessed then with the depleting ozone layer). In fourth grade, we learned a song called "Driving Miss Lazy," which included the lyrics, "You say you need a ride, but there's a voice inside: 'Put on those old walkin' shoes!' ... If you must take a car, make sure it's really far, and pick up some friends on the way! Cause drivin' 'Miss Lazy' is sometimes just crazy. Stop drivin' 'Miss Lazy' today!" Another song went, in part, "Every time you spray a can, toss a fridge, or charge a fan, CFCs and halon escape. They float up to the atmosphere, eating ozone and it's clear—burning rays of sun seal our fate. We're destroying a planet that we take for granted!"

I haven't read any of the books or many of the articles about how the earth is dying, even though I had an early example in my maternal grandfather, the first person I was very close to who died, who began growing vegetables organically in his backyard after reading Rachel Carson's *Silent Spring*. (I've been given *Silent Spring* no fewer than three times and I haven't read it once; when my grandfather died, I sobbed for a week straight and then didn't cry again for the four following years.) I am growing a vegetable garden—tomatoes, squash, kale, potatoes, peppers, chard, melons, broccoli, peas, beans, herbs—but the part of me that worries about environmental apocalypse also wonders if I am really working on food security, or simply offering myself a way to feel closer to my grandfather, who is gone, and closer to the earth before it's gone too, and I am gone with it.

I haven't read any of the books about how the earth is dying because I don't understand how I would eat breakfast or clean the cat's litter box or go to work after reading even one of those books, and I need to eat breakfast and clean the cat's litter box and go to work in order to keep a roof over my head in the here and now. It's a pressing problem but one that isn't fixable with any kind of personal consumer choice—it's only fixable on the type of scale that seems politically impossible. Two years ago, for example, when Canada purchased the floundering Trans Mountain pipeline from Kinder Morgan for $4.5 billion, Prime Minister Justin Trudeau justified the decision by telling *Bloomberg News*, "in order to be able to protect our environment, we do need to be able to have a strong and growing economy." It's a phrase he said right after he'd said the inverse—"creating a strong growing economy for the long term also requires the environment"—which he sandwiched between a callback to the way he was raised and an exhortation not to embrace all-or-nothing thinking. I'm not sure what reading best-sellers about the climate apocalypse can do to rewire Western democracy; a 600-page tome about the icebergs melting may have less impact than 600 paper airplanes saying WE CAN'T EAT OR BREATHE OR DRINK MONEY sailing towards the stage where the Bloomberg reporter chuckles conspiratorially with our sleeves-rolled-up nonsense-talker of a prime minister.

When I was a child, all of the possible options presented for continuing existence post-death bumped up against the reality, driven home by my music teacher, that the earth itself would eventually become uninhabitable, and the universe itself would expire. Unfathomably terrifying. Necessarily incomprehensible. But it was only when I reached my mid-twenties that the seeds of climate fears planted in the nineties suddenly and finally germinated. I still wanted to personally live forever and bring everyone I cared about on a metaphorical life raft, but the life raft began to feel less and less metaphorical.

The first time my partner, Will, and I met, in a coffee shop on Main Street in Vancouver, he asked me if I felt like the world was getting irredeemably, unfixably worse. Donald Trump hadn't yet been elected US president, but he would be within the next few years; the Western world seemed addicted to oil, and to outsourcing conflict in order to plunder necessary resources. Socially, some things seemed to be getting better—but what good was that if climate change would exacerbate the world's unfairness, including the ways in which it doled out death and prolonged life? Will didn't share my anxieties around his own mortality, but it seemed like we'd been thinking, or feeling, similar things. Then again, we both wondered if every generation had felt like this—an ego-driven worry that theirs would be the last generation, that the world was finally ending. Miller believed the apocalypse was nigh in 1844, and I remember standing on a frozen beach on December 31, 1999, skeptical but mildly afraid that the worst predictions about Y2K would come true. Was the worry reasonable, in 2012, a few steps closer than 1999 to climate disaster—and the year of the doomsday scare that arose from New Age misinterpretations of the Mayan calendar? Or was it just more of the same?

IN AN ESSAY FOR THE New York Times—a well-written essay featuring the kind of snark that leaves a metallic taste in your mouth—novelist Dara Horn skewers the tendency of Silicon Valley billionaires to want to "solv[e] 'the problem of death.'" Women who work in this area, she writes, tend to focus on "curbing age-related pathology." They wish for people to be less sick and in pain but take a more holistic view of the importance of aging and death to life. By contrast, men who fund and work in life extension studies are the type to decide they are going to live until they are hundreds of years old, melting time "into a vortex of solipsism."

Raymond Kurzweil, for one, eats a specialized million-dollar-a-year diet and thinks we'll soon do away with disease and aging and live forever by somehow uploading part of our consciousnesses to the cloud. The guy who popularized buttered coffee in North America had his bone marrow extracted so that his stem cells could be reinjected into his joints, spinal cord, cerebral fluid, scalp, face, and genitals; his goal is to live to 180. Peter Thiel, who has funded several life extension companies, is so uncomfortable with the idea of dying that he referred to it as "the ideology of the inevitability of the death of every individual" in an interview with the New Yorker.

Women, Horn writes, don't have this kind of hubris because they are used to caring for the bodies and lives of others; women are daily immersed "in the fragility of human life and the endless effort required to sustain it" and are thus more accustomed to thinking about bodily vulnerability, including the ultimate vulnerability of death. The stunted-maturity men of Silicon Valley need to learn something caregivers know innately, she writes: "You are a body, only a body, and nothing more."

It's an argument that reminds me of something Julia Cooper writes in her book The Last Word: "Death is what gives life its impetus, its very breath." But what do you do when you don't feel that way? To borrow another metaphor from the book: What do you do when death feels less like the seasoning for life, and more like the main course? I have played the imaginative game of telescoping my life forward and forward and forward to try to induce some sense of sadness or selfishness for extending the telescope too far, but every time, I find myself utterly comfortable with the problems of living forever, more comfortable than I am with the idea of dying. And I am, every day, grateful to be alive even though I know, as Horn guesses the Silicon Valleyites don't, all about bodily vulnerability. I know it's selfish to want to not die; I know what it means to carry and care for another human being. I know all of this, yet I still feel the same way I did when I was eight and absolutely terrified of dying.

I find myself, sometimes, walking close to external walls, like a rat, to lessen the chance of something falling catastrophically on my head. I blanch every time I get into a car, because driving and suicide are the two ways someone my age, gender, race, and socioeconomic class are most likely to die. I cry every time I think of someone I love dying. I cry when people I don't know die, particularly senselessly, because someone somewhere extinguished the only time that person got on earth. I feel the same way I did when I was eight, and it's not just selfish.

When I google how to deal with a fear of death so bad that it takes away from daily life, what comes up are Psychology Today articles asserting that this fear often crops up as a major theme in middle age. The common wisdom is that fear of death exposes different, underlying fears, and the solution is to adjust your life so that it feels more meaningful. I have no other real fears, because I am willing to live through anything that isn't dying. Maybe I laugh with Horn but land with Thiel for a gender-related reason. I'm not a man, but maybe I have the hubris of one.

ANTHONY STORR DEFINES THE GURUS he covers in Feet of Clay as inherently narcissistic. They become gurus, he writes, after experiencing a "dark night of the soul," followed by an emerging dawn of insight. Storr argues that this process of chaos followed by insight is something shared by artists and creators. Many gurus, he writes, lead isolated childhoods with few friends—another commonality, besides an obsession with endings, that I share with them. The difference between gurus and artists, according to Storr, is that gurus find certainty and comfort in their insight, maintaining it through faith and delusion and by convincing others, while artists never reach that same level of internal or external certainty. So artists worry the world is getting worse and worse and maybe ending, and then we wonder if that fear is part of the human condition—or if it's narcissistic, or a reasonable reaction to climate change, or an intense and dizzying mix of all of the above. The truth is that I fear death and endings, and I always will. I study believers, gurus, and religion because I'll never be a believer myself. I crave certainty, but I'll never find it; in a way that is more seeking and less Ozymandias, this fear will probably be the driving force behind much of my writing, and art, for the rest of my life.

The problem of death is a problem that feels both fundamental and unresolvable. Although I would be better off if the fear didn't rule me, it most likely always will. The fear won't save me from death, because death is inevitable. All I can hope is that I won't die soon. All I can do is accept that I will sometimes be so afraid of dying that I take half an hour or an hour or a day off living, and then move on.

erika

ERIKA IS TURNING FORTY. She's probably going to be really annoying about it on Twitter all year long. Something big usually happens to her every ten years. When she was nineteen, she finally started university. That really changed her life. When she was twenty-nine, turning thirty, she moved to Vancouver and started grad school. She doesn't know exactly what form the change will take this time, but she feels like she has decisions to make about the next phase of her career.

Erika grew up in a townhouse in north Edmonton, not the worst part of north Edmonton. Erika was twelve when her family moved into the townhouse. She'd lived in Winnipeg until then. They moved to Edmonton because her mom couldn't get work in Winnipeg and her dad wasn't paying child support. When Erika thinks about Edmonton, she thinks about it in the summertime, so it's all glow-y, in the way that the Prairies get. In the winter, it was pretty dire.

The townhouse was a three-bedroom with a basement, and her room was in the basement. Upstairs was her grandmother, her brother, her mom, and the bathroom. Erika's room spanned half of the basement, but her room was also storage space. Her family never threw anything away. When she first moved in, she put up posters of Christian Bale and Christian Slater, but her TV was sort of her decoration. There were parts of her room that she didn't have much control over. It was packed with furniture, it was messy, but it had a TV.

Erika didn't feel comfortable at home. The townhouse felt crowded, because Erika and her brother were both getting older, and her mother's mental health and her grandmother's mental health weren't great. Erika's grandmother had had polio as a child, so she had a really hard time walking, and she didn't leave her room very often. Her brother had rage issues. Erika tried to be out of the house as much as possible. In high school, she spent days at a time sleeping over at friends' houses. In grade twelve, she had a friend move in with her. It was way too many people for that small house, but she does have warm memories of her mom making breakfast for them, or of having people over.

Erika has mostly dated men, but she's always been attracted to women, and sometimes that expressed itself in the form of really super intense friendships, and sometimes in straight-up desire. Erika grew up in a really permissive atmosphere. Her closest uncle is gay. If she'd told her mom she's bisexual, her mom probably wouldn't have had any problem with it. But she's never told her, just because she's never really thought it was her mom's business. Erika's sexuality wasn't the thing that made her need to get out of her house. It was her mom's mental health issues, and her relationships with her mom and her brother.

When Erika was in grade twelve she got really heavily involved in chat culture, and fell in love with a boy on the internet. Erika remembers logging on to the internet for the first time. The sound it made. The first boy she corresponded with on the internet was a guy named Chris, in Dublin. They had long, late-night chats. He sent Erika a picture of himself, and it broke her email. She had to get her mom to call their internet service provider to purge the email from her inbox. Erika was really involved in the Sailor Moon fandom and had one of the first Sailor Moon fan websites. She also discovered cybersex, which made life in her small house very complicated. She had cybersex with girls, boys, everyone. It was fun. It was like writing a thousand collaborative, smutty sex novels. Sexuality was kind of in the background for Erika, but sex was very much in the foreground of her life.

Erika's family didn't have money for her to go to university, and she didn't understand how student loans worked. She thought she couldn't go to university, so she didn't go to university. Instead, she went to Missouri to live with her internet boyfriend and his family. Her boyfriend wasn't very much older than her. He was nineteen and she was seventeen. He paid for her to fly from Alberta to Missouri.

Erika remembers arriving at his house in Missouri. At first it was weird, because they were kids, and they'd made this bizarre decision. But she also remembers being relaxed for the first time in her life. She'd had a cat growing up, despite being deathly allergic to cats. When she got to Missouri and moved into her boyfriend's mother's house, she could breathe, literally and figuratively. Her first visit she was there for four months.

When she went back to Alberta, things with her family had gotten way worse. She ended up leaving again, and she and her boyfriend got an apartment together for six months. Erika left and came back, left and came back. Until her mother sold the house. In her memory, that time feels like it lasted ten years, but thinking back, it was a short and compact period of time. Erika's boyfriend really wanted her to marry him. They got engaged at one point. He gave her a ring. And she was like, "Uhh, no."

By mid-1999, Erika had figured out that she just needed her mom to sign a form for her to get a student loan. She enrolled, and she thought, *Well, I'll go to university and maybe see where this relationship goes after that.* At university, Erika took a bus ride with her friend Jamie. She remembers it so clearly. They were sitting at the back of the bus, talking about whether Erika should break up with her boyfriend. She told Jamie that she was with the boyfriend in part because she was worried that no one else would ever love her, and Jamie looked at her and said, "Erika, that's not a reason to be in a relationship."

Erika had spent every minute that she wasn't at high school online. That's what connected her to her first boyfriend, and it's also where she had a lot of transformational experiences, where she was able to express herself in ways that she wasn't able to express herself outside of the internet, and make friendships with people who were just really kind and interested in the same things she was. The internet also allowed her to live outside of her body, and outside of the pressures of normative femininity that Erika felt in her day-to-day life. Erika cannot undersell how beautiful the internet was when it first started, when it first became really popular. It was a worldwide web of nerdy kids who couldn't have good relationships, kicking off their shoes and diving into each other. They were all their most playful, uninhibited, happy selves.

3

ON BEING BIPOLAR

AT AGE EIGHTEEN, I WAS DIAGNOSED BIPOLAR II. Less than a decade later, sometime in my mid-to-late twenties, I participated in a study that sought to glean insights from "high-functioning" bipolar people—presumably to figure out why we were high-functioning, and if we had anything to share that could help others become high-functioning, too.

The study took place in a little room in a low-slung building that seemed like it was built in the seventies. (This feels true of many of the buildings where psychological studies take place.) A grad student, maybe a bit younger than me, administered the study. She was cleaner-cut, normal-seeming, slim. We could have had a friend or two in common; we could have ended up on the same coed dodgeball team. At the beginning of the interview, she consulted with an older man before we entered the room. And then she proceeded to ask me questions about my diagnosis and mental health history. When she got to the part of the survey about hallucinations, she seemed apologetic, ready to skip it—bipolar people can but don't always experience hallucinations and/or psychosis, and it's less common with bipolar II than bipolar I.

"Oh," I said, "we will need to go through those." After I answered: yes, I'd experienced visual hallucinations while ill, and yes, I'd experienced auditory hallucinations while ill, she excused herself and went to consult, a second time, with the older psychologist. When she came back, I could tell that I had gone from being one type of person, in her perception, to another type of person. The wrong type of person. The type of person we place in a separate category in order to quarantine whatever it is that makes them abnormal and a bit frightening. (I'm using the word "abnormal" here colloquially—but also because abnormal psychology is the branch that studies mental disorders, of which I have several.)

During the period of time when I was hallucinating, I was also living in circumstances that the woman who was interviewing me probably would have found appalling. In the winter, my then-partner and I wore toques and hoodies to bed because it was too cold not to. At the very end of my bachelor's degree, which coincided with the peak of one of his drinking binges, I woke up to write my final exam and had to step over him, as he was passed out on the floor and surrounded by broken glass, to get to the coffee maker. I was taking lithium. I saw birds in the corners of our rooms—one owl, in particular, recurred. I heard a low, echoing voice. I knew these were hallucinations, and I lived with them just I like I lived with my boyfriend's alcoholism and the broken glass on the floor. Many years later, now that I am stable and my life is stable, I can sometimes still be picked out by normal people, ones who can sense that I've experienced periods of poverty and illness. Other times, I can pass for the type of person who has never experienced these things—and then, if they come up, they come as a shock. I'm not sure what's better or worse.

WHEN THE MEDIA TALKS ABOUT MENTAL ILLNESS, the conversation is usually framed around reducing stigma—#LetsTalk about mental health—and around the costs to employers, as half a million workers are out sick with mental health issues weekly, translating into a $50 billion hit to the economy. Focusing on stigma cleanly removes the personal economic costs of mental illness from the conversation; focusing on costs to employers frames the illness in terms of productivity, what one owes one's employer.

For sixty percent of people diagnosed bipolar, what one owes one's employer is a moot point, because sixty percent of people diagnosed bipolar are unemployed. Stephen Fry's 2006 documentary, The Secret Life of the Manic Depressive, is mostly filtered through his personal experience as he seeks to get to the root of the causes and effects of his bipolar disorder— and as he struggles to decide if he'll take medication for it. But he also speaks to other people, including a doctor who works half time, a young woman who can't work at all, and celebrities for whom work is presented as less of an economic problem and more of a creative expression or outlet. Fry works. Fry works almost compulsively, almost as if he is a shark who will die if he ever stops moving. I might do this, too, even if I weren't currently the main earner for my very moderately middle-class household, which includes my partner and my toddler and my tabby cat (and an uncountable number of what I at first thought were wolf spiders but are actually "giant house spiders"). I live with a feeling of constant stress that began in childhood, stress that if I don't work at or near max capacity, I will lose the roof over my head. In childhood, I had no control, no way of stemming the tide of calls from collection agencies, calls from the bank. The first thing I did when I made real money of my own was not to save for a Game Boy or new comic books; it was to buy the food I wanted to eat.

When I spun out at eighteen, I was between my first and second years of university, and had come home to Hamilton instead of staying in Guelph. My parents had split up in my first semester after the day-lighting of an affair between my mom and my best friend's father, and the composition of my family and my best friend's family had shifted into a temporary, liminal space—as if we had been suspended before we could move forward. My mother and my best friend's father were renting a small house by the highway in Winona, just south of Hamilton, on Lake Ontario. My dad and my brother were still in our childhood home, where I went; that house was a stone's throw from my best friend's house, and that summer we all, except for the two in Winona, had regular barbecues in our backyard. Through a buddy of hers from the bar, my mother got me a job at a Hamilton Parks & Rec location near her house. Ten-hour days at the beginning of the season progressing to twelve-hour days later on. Mowing lawns, clearing firepits, picking up garbage, directing parking traffic during events. I had a second part-time job at the video rental store I'd worked at near the end of high school, so I was working anywhere from ten to sixteen hours a day when I went off the rails.

While everyone around me—my dad, my brother, my best friend, her family—seemed to have been slowly processing the affair and its after-math, I felt like I'd returned from the freedom of university life to the direct, unrelenting pressures of life with my mother. Whatever progress I'd made at school evaporated; my mother wanted me to stay over at her place after work to avoid the drive home, and if I relented, she'd get progressively drunker as she complained about how shitty my dad was. We'd never talked about the affair, which had started when I was living at home and working at my best friend's father's store, and which I'd attempted to confront my mother about in high school. We'd never talked about her drinking. I was angry and resentful, but my anger was a chiminea to my mother's forest fire. One night, when I yelled at her that I couldn't take it anymore, she yelled back. I've blanked out what, exactly, she said, but I remember later thinking that it was as if she'd used the years she'd been my parent solely to hone the sharpest and most painful insults. I also remember later cautioning myself, based on what she'd said, that I couldn't trust her, that I'd have to give up thinking of her as a mother, my mother. I ran out of her house and down the lane, the sound of highway traffic audible beyond the noise barrier. I heard my mother's door open; I heard her car start. I looked around. I could jump into a drainage ditch or sprint to the end of the road and hide behind a concrete barrier. I went for the barrier. I could hear my mom driving around, which terrified me because she was drunk. I called my dad, who came and picked me up. I never stayed at my mother's house in Winona again.

I tried to maintain the pace of my life for a few weeks after that. The confluence of my jobs already meant that I wasn't always getting as much sleep as I needed. I started sleeping even less. I went to a party in the west end of Hamilton, got drunk, and had no way to get home. The buses had stopped running. Instead of taking a cab, I made an overnight eleven-kilometre trek home along the rail trail that connects Hamilton and Dundas, arriving just as the sun was coming up and my dad was leaving for work. I got into a fender-bender on the highway driving home one day, and then I got into another accident while picking up my co-worker; the other car's hubcap went rolling across the road, like in the movies, all noise suspended except for the sound of metal spinning and then falling on concrete like a top. I drank and smoked and cheated on my boyfriend with someone I'd had a crush on in high school; I promised that boy the world. On the phone with my boyfriend, I felt as though I'd promised away too many worlds. I could no longer keep anything together. When I realized that my mother was not a mother like other people had, I began to cycle between grief and self-recrimination, wondering why I was not lovable, wondering why my own mother could not love me. I couldn't think straight. I thought maybe it would calm my nerves to take a shot of my father's whisky. I had already taken an Ativan, which I'd been pre-scribed for one of my anxiety disorders. I took a shot, and then another shot, and then everything I was holding tight began to unravel. I emptied the bottle of whisky and took the rest of the pills. My boyfriend, the one who'd later become an alcoholic himself, called 911 and an ambulance arrived at my house just as my dad and brother did, too.

I wasn't kept overnight at the hospital. The nurse, whom I'd irritated by neglecting to stop keening about what a fuck-up I was, handed me a pamphlet for Alcoholics Anonymous as I was shuffled out of the hospital the very night I'd arrived. I never went back to the Parks & Rec job but couldn't quit working outright—I'd signed a lease on a place in Guelph and needed to make rent. Very shortly after my nadir, I got a part-time job at a grocery store as a checkout clerk.

When I think about mental illness, I think first about Virginia Woolf placing her hand into a pocket of rocks. I think about movies or shows I've seen where depression is depicted as a series of long, slow-moving days, stuck in one's home, maybe breaking the monotony by heading to the corner store in a bathrobe in search of cigarettes and ice cream. (When I think about mania, I think about rich young men taking cocaine and driving fast and apparently covetably ugly small cars.) Only after a few beats do I think about myself—my life oriented around working through illness, an economic crisis never far off. Perhaps this anxiety is protective; perhaps I've never been so badly off, maybe all those mornings I've shoved my legs off the side of the bed to propel my body out of it wouldn't have been possible if I were more ill, truly ill. Depictions of serious mental illness seem to exist without a middle—celebrities whose lows are captured by paparazzi, men with shopping carts under bridges. But the truth is most of our breakdowns are private, and if we talk about them at all, we talk about them after we've stabilized. If you're not stable, people talk about you, for you, instead.

BIPOLAR DISORDER HAS BEEN ROMANTICIZED IN POP CULTURE. It's presented as better, perhaps more inherently interesting, than depression, which we see as a disease that renders already waifish young women thinner and sadder, or middle-aged men more bloated, full of beer and ice cream. Like schizophrenia, bipolar disorder is generally embodied onscreen by men— though it affects women at more or less the same rate.

Bipolar disorder is depicted as a font of creativity, fun, and terrible choices. Virginia Woolf, van Gogh, Stephen Fry, Carrie Fisher, Charlie Sheen, Britney Spears, Chris Brown, Catherine Zeta-Jones, Lou Reed, Kim Novak, Edvard Munch, Marilyn Monroe. If you're famous and bipolar, your name will grace googleable lists, many devoid of any kind of context. You can be known for succeeding despite your diagnosis, or you can be known for the train wreck you make of your life and career. The only way you can stake a claim to your own story is to tell it yourself, like Fry did.

The problem with sharing your personal story—or the story of being bipolar filtered through your experience—is that people who don't share your diagnosis may essentialize the disorder, placing your experience at the pinnacle of their pyramid of understanding of what it means, in general, to be bipolar. And the further problem is that it's easiest to package your illness in the way that it is already culturally understood—and maybe the cultural understanding even begins to shape your understanding of yourself.

The end result is that the story of being bipolar—an illness with ups and downs, which offers a narrative more easily than illnesses without—is one where, often, the manic protagonist must wrestle his euphoria to the ground for the sake of his sanity. When you are manic, the understanding is that you enjoy your mania. It's only the mess, afterwards, that provokes reflection and a tidy combination of SSRIs and mood stabilizers.

This has not been my experience of mania. Or maybe it has, and I like it less. The broad truth about suicidality and bipolar disorder is that people with it are about thirty times more likely than the general public, and twice as likely as people with unipolar depression, to kill themselves. The broad truth about me is that I never want to die, and that if I did kill myself, it would happen accidentally, while I was hypomanic.

Adjacent to the list I can recite of famous people with bipolar disorder is another list, a list of non-famous people, friends and acquaintances. I won't list them—their stories are not mine to tell. Two of them died by overdose, one accidentally and one not as accidentally. Both were people who maybe found it easier to care deeply about others than themselves.

When I'm up late at night, wanting to sleep but pushing sleep off because I am afraid of death, one or the other will come floating to the top of my mind, and I will think, Shit. Because I don't want either of them to be dead. And I don't want to die, either. Not ever, and definitely not accidentally. The night that I was briefly hospitalized—the night that was a culmination of terrible days and weeks, the night that led to my diagnosis—is a blur with pinpricks of clarity. But I remember very acutely the feeling that led me to down, by shots, and then all at once, an entire bottle of whisky as well as what remained of my Ativan prescription—like I had, sometime earlier, swallowed firecrackers and would give anything, do anything, to put them out.

I don't associate mania with creativity, or fun, or clarity; I associate it with an abundance of energy that seems like it needs no fuel but that will end up using me for its fuel. When it comes, now, I prepare for it as if I live on a cottage by the ocean and a storm is about to blow through. I don't think that my experience of bipolar disorder should be read as bipolar's new urtext, but I do wonder why I feel such a chasm between the way that the illness is so often depicted and my experience of it. I wonder if there is something about me that is lacking, essentially unfun, as dull and bland as baby cereal. Or if, when I am asked to help explain why I am "high-functioning" and other people are not, the answer is fear. Fear of poverty and fear of dying. Can fear keep you safe? Or will fear kill me early, just in a different way?

ESMÉ WEIJUN WANG WRITES VERY MOVINGLY about being one of the good sick. Her doctors are initially reluctant to switch her diagnosis from bipolar disorder to schizoaffective disorder, bipolar type, because schizoaffective disorder "has a gloomier prognosis and stigma than bipolar disorder does." During an earlier hospitalization, Wang had noticed that there was even a hierarchy on the ward: the two women at the bottom of the hierarchy were the women who were very clearly, to the other patients, schizophrenic. Wang, who had not yet experienced psychosis, treated schizophrenic Pauline "like a contagion." Perhaps, she writes, she sensed the possibility of psychosis "thrumming in [herself] even then."

There are many benefits that one gets, being the good sick. And there are compromises one makes to remain the good sick. And then there is the fear of becoming the contagion.

I've been asked several times why I chose not to come out as nonbinary to my OB/GYN and the other medical professionals I interacted with when I was pregnant. There is the simple answer, which is that I didn't feel comfortable doing so, and the more complex answer: I knew that the hormones that would come along with pregnancy and birth, and the not-sleeping that would come along with having a newborn, had the potential to throw me into a manic crisis. ("Women with bipolar disorder are at a very high risk for having a much more severe episode of illness in relationship to childbirth, often with psychotic symptoms like hallucinations or delusions," researcher Ian Jones says in the Stephen Fry doc. "And really these episodes can be some of the most severe episodes of illness that we see in psychiatric practice.") I didn't have alternatives for what, other than "mother," I could call myself, and I didn't know if I could find trans-affirming care; on the flip side, I had a very strong urge to be as candid as possible about being bipolar so that I could be streamed into emergency mental health care if it became necessary. While being candid, though, I also wanted to appear as stable, as normal, as possible. I needed to begin as one of the good sick so that if I became, over the course of my pregnancy or after birth, one of the bad sick, I would have the best chance of accessing the kind of care that might save me. To be the good sick, it helps to be articulate, to make the right kind of eye contact, to check off as many privileges as you can. I did not know if I could afford to be both non-binary and bipolar. So I compromised.

WHEN YOU ARE THE BAD SICK, you become a cautionary tale. My great-aunt is a cautionary tale. She was first bipolar, and then got dementia, and then, most recently, cancer. I don't know my great-aunt except through photos; she was the youngest of three sisters and very outgoing in her youth, but by the time I was growing up she didn't like to leave her apartment. I learned she had cancer when my cousin posted about it on Facebook. My cousin wrote first that she was upset to have unexpectedly learned of her aunt's illness, and then, two days later, that "every disease is mental first," and "everything is mind over matter," and "[e]verything is about vibration." I wondered at what stage my cousin thought that my great-aunt should have vibrated herself out of illness. I thought a series of angrier things.

If you lined up my cousin and me, my dad, my grandmother, my great-aunt, you would clearly see we were all related. Variations on a theme. If my cousin can assign vibrational blame to my great-aunt's illnesses, maybe that helps her to not see herself in them. When my great-aunt was diagnosed with dementia, a disease my great-grandmother had as well, I thought, Well, my bipolar disorder isn't as bad as hers. I thought, I do the crossword. I did not build my rationalizations a spiritual structure and I did not invite them to stay, but I thought them and I felt them.

Like my initial desire to distance myself from my great-aunt's illnesses, I don't feel proud of the compromises I've made to try to be, and to appear to be, one of the good sick. But I'm sure if I was faced with the same choices at the same points in my life, I'd make the same decisions over again. I do worry about the way that illnesses like bipolar disorder are rendered visible, via personal narrative and through productivity statistics. I worry that we understand illness and wellness as something that we hold and foster as individuals, and that this masks the extent to which social conditions like racism, sexism, homophobia, overwork, classism, and eviscerated social safety nets trigger and exacerbate them. This is the dark side of gleaning what we can from the narratives of the good sick in order to give better "tools" to the bad sick, to make them "higher-functioning"—is the idea to improve a person's quality of life, or to render them a better worker? It's also why I tap out, each year, of participating in campaigns like Bell's #LetsTalk: they place the onus on the unwell to share their stories for nickels and dimes while raising brand recognition. Understandably, people share what is safe for them to share; I doubt Bell will chip in on my mortgage if I no longer appear quite as employable because I regularly saw an imaginary owl for a steady period in my early twenties. The result is a sanitized portrayal of illness that does little to shorten psychiatric wait times for people, like me, who rely on provincial health care to seek mental health treatment.

Sometimes, I dream about how wealthy I would need to be to take a break from feeling the fear that propels me to remain stable. I don't dream about not being bipolar, because I don't know where my self ends and where the illness begins, and if there is even really a difference. I don't even know what I would dream to render the divisions between good sick and bad sick unnecessary, to make it so that we all get to remain people, without reducing some of us to possibility models—or, worse, sacrificing us to quarantine and cautionary tale.

deneige

DENEIGE WAS BORN IN 1990. She's twenty-nine and uses the term "queer," mostly. She also likes "dyke" a lot, so she uses that too. Deneige grew up in Coaldale and Chin, Alberta. She went to school in Lethbridge because that's where the International Baccalaureate program was. Coaldale had maybe a population of 5,000 when Deneige lived there, and Chin had about 60 people. She moved to Chin when she was about ten, just for a couple years. Her mother's second husband had a house there. She and her mother moved back to Coaldale when they split up.

Coaldale is very religious. It's a bit of a Bible belt, with a high German Mennonite population. In the surrounding communities, there are quite a few folks who are Mormon as well. Coaldale has more than a dozen churches, which is a lot for 5,000 people. There were two elementary schools when Deneige was growing up. One school was mostly farm kids, and the other was mostly town kids. Deneige went to the one with the farm kids. The elementary school that she went to had Wednesday afternoon Bible studies with the local Mennonites, even though it was a public school. Her mom was a hairdresser. Her stepfather worked in construction. She hasn't spoken with her father since she was twelve, so she's not sure about him. Last she heard, he was running a cult out of his basement.

Deneige was raised non-denominationally, because her mother was raised Jehovah's Witness, but her father was Mormon, and her father's family was all Catholic French Canadian. Deneige isn't a believer. But she had an acute fear of going to hell. It definitely shaped her. But she's pretty staunchly atheist now.

Deneige felt very strongly that she didn't belong in her hometown. Deneige's mother was concerned about her and her sister's potential drug use, given that they were in a small community with not a lot to do. So they cleaned the dance studio in exchange for ballet and dance classes, and Deneige trained in ballet for fourteen years. Deneige has never really been a small person, which was fine at her studio, but she'd go to dance competitions and the adjudicators would say things like, "No ballet dancer should be over ninety pounds." She didn't have many friends within her dance studio communities. She didn't have a lot of friends in school, either. She was very anxious and depressed for a lot of her life. When she was in grade seven, she stopped talking to people, period. She read instead. She did her school work, went to dance class, and read a novel a day.

Growing up, Deneige had no clue she was queer. She knew one couple who were gay men. They've always been out, but it's a "don't ask, don't tell" situation. They didn't really display a lot of public affection. She didn't even realize that it was a possibility for women. Deneige came out to her family when was twenty-one or twenty-two. A lot of people in high school told her she was a lesbian, or called her a lesbian. But it wasn't until she moved to Vancouver that she had the space to figure life out.

Queer theorist Didier Eribon wrote an entire book on insult as the making of the gay self, and how we get penned in by language that precedes us. Deneige teaches at Emily Carr University of Art + Design, and one of the essays she teaches is on heterosexual interpellation, which is an idea that comes from Louis Althusser. Althusser's philosophy basically says that nobody is an individual or a free subject; we are all subject to ideology, and informed and made by what preceded us, as well as our cultural surroundings. Eribon takes up his ideas and extends them. For Eribon, the space of heterosexual interpellation shows that we are formed as queer subjects potentially before we even know that we are. We're named before we name ourselves, in many ways, but this naming is often meant to be derogatory, meant as an insult. There's a way in which one comes to know and understand oneself as queer through this language—but then Eribon also talks about the complexity of what it means to have been a child who has used this language against others, and what it means to come to realize that you inhabit that which is "ugly." Deneige finds this really helpful. It's been instrumental in terms of thinking about how certain ideologies function in our culture right now, and how they might be open to different modes of change.

Deneige was eighteen when she left Alberta. She graduated high school and then two months later, she was living in Vancouver. In Lethbridge, she had a great art teacher who encouraged her to apply to art school, and she ended up at Emily Carr. She was very out in Vancouver before she was out to her family. She was chairing the queer caucus of her student union at provincial meetings, and her family had no clue. Her friend almost drunkenly outed her to her sister once.

Living in Vancouver, getting to meet queer folks of all sorts of ages and experiences, and starting to understand a more embodied history, has felt wonderful to Deneige. She's met people who were institutionalized when they were young, and has learned of the different ways they define family now. It would feel too simplistic to say that there are massive differences between different generations of queer people. We've actually lost some of the intergenerational connections that we used to have, in ways that can be quite detrimental in terms of not having and maintaining our own histories. If one's life is illegal, community comes from specific underground spaces where everybody congregates. That space of younger folks getting to learn from their elders doesn't exist in the same way. Queer people in Canada have done a fantastic amount of activism to be recognized as legal subjects under Canadian law. We're more accepted into the culture as it exists; our cultures have pressed up against its norms to make a bit of space for us. Many things have been made possible, but it's also shifted how we relate to each other as a community and a safety net.

The younger generation fucks with gender in ways Deneige never really saw in her own community, which feels exciting. When Deneige thinks about queerness today, she thinks about negotiating a kind of queer politics between an anti-assimilationist position versus a position of trying to make space within the system. But maybe that's sort of a false dichotomy. Or too dialectical. There's been so much work already done for inclusion, and a lot more that needs to be done, but the bit of space that has been opened up has allowed people to survive, to fuck around with things in exciting ways, to play around with gender as an embodiment and a construction. The conversations she sees her students having are radically different from those she used to have.

But then it's also cultural. She still feels very different in Vancouver than in Alberta. Some of that has to do with her queerness. She goes to see her family once a year, and it's always bad by the end. Her family are political conservatives. She doesn't have a sense of family belonging. She was the first person in her family to go to university, let alone complete graduate school, and then teach. There's a class schism.

Often Deneige is like, "Why hasn't shit changed?" But last spring, she happened to have a student who was queer and grew up in Lethbridge and went to the same high school. Talking with her felt quite incredible to Deneige. There's now a Gay–Straight Alliance in the school. Thinking about it, she's amazed. Nobody was out in her time. There were a couple guys who were pretty flamboyantly gay, and people knew, but it was still never an explicitly spoken thing. Deneige's student just seemed more comfortable in herself. It's good to know that exists at the school now.

And Deneige appreciates seeing non-binary identity emerge and flourish. The younger queer people in her life often assume that she is non-binary, but she's taken up maybe a different sort of mode, where she knows she fails at femininity, but she intentionally wants to fail at it, wants to make possible more ways of being a woman. She knows she's always done her gender wrong, but she doesn't not feel like a woman. That's a different thing. It's a rich conversation to have, to say, "No, I intentionally identify as a woman, in order to mess with that." That's what makes her able to not hate herself for the rest of her life. To embrace the failure.

april

APRIL WAS BORN IN 1989. She usually identifies as queer. If she says "bisexual," some people think that means trans-exclusive. April grew up in Kanata, Ontario. When she was a young kid, Kanata was its own city. Later, Kanata was one of the small towns that got amalgamated into Ottawa. But it still felt very closed-minded and conservative. There weren't a lot of resources in Kanata. You had to go to Ottawa, the "big city," to get stuff if you needed it.

April went to Catholic school. Ninety percent of the students were white, and queer identities were not discussed. She couldn't get resources outside of school, and she couldn't get them at school, because Jesus would've hated her, or something.

April's grandparents are Catholic. Her father grew up Catholic, and his sister got pregnant when she was eighteen and kept the kid. Next thing they knew, April's father was spending his entire life trying to make sure his kids didn't screw up like that. April didn't want to make any mistakes in front of her dad. Growing up, she tried to maintain an image of perfection. She graduated with honours, the highest grades in all her classes. She went to Ontario Catholic Youth Leadership camp, which she had to apply to and submit essays for. She went even though she's not religious at all.

In her house and at school, April felt like she could be a variant of herself but not fully herself. At school, with her friend group, she was open and honest and talkative, but she also planned music for their Masses. She couldn't talk openly about feeling confused about her sexuality.

April's mom hates the way sex ed is taught in Catholic school, so when April's school sent home a letter in grade four informing her parents that the school was going to teach her class sex ed, April's mom got super hands-on and had what April remembers as an over-the-top, in-depth conversation about sex. April found it haunting and traumatizing. And their relationship was strange, because April experienced really bad mental health throughout her teens. She was a cutter. When her mom found out she was cutting, she said, "What did I do wrong?" April didn't want her mom to think she'd damaged her.

At school, April took religion every single year. She can tell you now, all the different Catholic components—the beatitudes, the Ten Commandments. She remembers internalizing that once you had sex, you were garbage. You were only supposed to have sex in the context of being married. If you were masculine, you could want sex all the time. It was the woman's job to stop it. April's lessons assumed that there were only two genders and that everyone was straight. April's grateful they taught sex ed at her school, but they didn't talk about sex outside of heterosexual sex for the purpose of procreation. April was probably the most educated of her friends, because her mom had sat her down and had that horrifying conversation. April's mom had explained that there were other options for sex and sexuality. She'd talked about masturbation, and that sex provided pleasure.

For April's entire teen years, she thought she was asexual, which she finds funny now. April didn't talk about her sexuality with anybody, even though her mom is a social worker on the public school board, and she works with a lot of trans kids and LGBTQ teens and youth. As a kid, April was petrified to tell her mother anything. April's father ended up realizing that April wasn't straight after he got into a debate with her on trans identities. April has close friends who are trans, and who transitioned in small towns outside Ottawa where there were no resources. When her father started saying something vaguely negative, April challenged him, and then he was actually speechless. He realized that she dated women. He realized she dated trans people. He hasn't brought it up with her since.

When April was eighteen, she didn't want to go to university, but her mother said, "Smart people go to university, so that's what you're doing." April went to school for about two years and hated it. She can't even remember what degree she was working on. She didn't want to keep going to school, and she knew it would be an issue for her parents, so she moved out of the house and in with her friends. The first thing her parents said to her was, "If you ever have a guy move in with you, you can't come back to live with us." April ended up in a situation where she needed a roommate, and her now-husband ended up moving in. At that moment, she knew: I don't get to go back now. She was about twenty.

April and her husband got married when she was twenty-four. April's husband had been the only partner that she'd ever been with until they decided to be polyamorous when April was twenty-six. She'd followed "being perfect" to the point where she'd chilled her ability to have a queer identity; some people around her saw it as "becoming" queer, as opposed to finally allowing herself to be queer.

The moment April and her husband went polyamorous, the world opened up to her. She met her friend Jess, who was transitioning, and April introduced Jess to her friend Mia, and Mia realized she was also trans, because she had somebody to talk to. April went from feeling like there were only straight, white, cis people in Kanata to "Here, meet the world." Starting sex work was incredibly freeing. For the first time in her entire life, she felt desirable. She got to see something totally different about herself that she hadn't seen before. It felt like her clients and the people she met in the kink community could see her outside of how her community saw her. Nobody in sex work says to her, "You're not queer enough, because you're married to a man." Nobody cares.

Coming out as polyamorous to her parents was harder than coming out as queer. April's mom was like, "Oh, okay, so you like more than just him, that's cool," and that was fine. But as soon as April was like, "Yeah, well, I'm going to pursue it," it was like, "Whoa, whoa, whoa. You can think it, you can feel it, but because you're married, you're not allowed to try it. You already did your thing. You aren't allowed to experiment with it, because you had to find one person and marry them." April's mom is getting more and more accepting as time goes on, but it's a learning curve. Whereas her father will never become more accepting. It seemed confusing to him, the prospect that April didn't care what genitals people had. It was too jarring.

Because of all this, April finds it hard to relate to younger people. She can't understand what they're saying, their newfangled lingo. When she looks at her parents' generation, a lot of them run the political landscape, and you get the message from them that "queer" isn't real and you're broken. And then if you talk to the younger kids, it's almost like you should be so empowered with your queerness that it defines you. The older generation is still conservative and so restricting, and then Gen Z is mad at millennials for not really doing more to fix things, but then, April feels like, *What were we supposed to do?*

April does sex work for a living. And she sees a therapist regularly. But she still doesn't quite know what to call herself. Learning about other people opened her eyes to other options and showed her that variations were okay. But at thirty, April feels like she's just now learning how to be herself. When she lived with her parents, it was like, "Discover who you are, to be that thing right away, so you can be perfect and get your life on track." Now her life is enjoying and discovering who she is, seeing who she wants to be, taking it at a pace that works for her and doing what she wants—not doing something for somebody else.

4

LIKE A BOY BUT NOT A BOY

AS MY LEFT LEG BUMPED THE EDGE OF THE COFFEE TABLE, a small wave of coffee curled up the side of my mug. Always clumsy, I seemed to have lost all sense of the boundaries of my body over the course of the first few months of pregnancy. The apartment I shared with my partner, Will, was a small one-bedroom in Little Italy in Montreal. Will is an avid gardener; the *Dracaena marginata* (Margie VII), which perched precariously on top of a Go board in our living room, was then my greatest nemesis: I knocked it off its centre and caught it as it fell an average of once a week.

It was odd to have lost grip of where I ended and the world began. It was odd and bruising in a different way that the world, always fuzzy on them, had lost sense of my conceptual boundaries, too. At about four or five months pregnant—a little rounder, but without, yet, a completely fleshed-out belly—I walked past a man and woman heading in the opposite direction on a street in the Plateau. The woman said in French, speaking to the man but looking directly at me, "You think they are boys, and then they are not boys."

I THINK A LOT ABOUT WHEN KIM KARDASHIAN WAS PREGNANT with North and the entire tabloid press was obsessed with her weight gain. My jeans got tight at six weeks along; when I went to a maternity store to find new pants, I lied and said I'd reached nine weeks. Size was not the only way in which I felt like an imposter: it seemed as though all the clothing on offer wished to emphasize every bit of my body I generally tried to downplay. "Boob shelves," bows, florals, form-fitting and empire-waist dresses. In the back, on the discount rack, I found two dark-coloured pairs of stretchy skinny jeans. They'd do. And I found shirts in the men's section at the various thrift stores in our neighbourhood.

On Instagram, I followed two different kinds of accounts that allowed me to see parts of myself reflected back. I followed accounts that cele-brated curvy bodies; these overwhelmingly featured feminine women. Stripped of clothes, the outline of my body resembled aspects of the variety of shapes and sizes that passed through my feed. I also followed accounts that displayed transmasculine and tomboy style. In clothes, this is what I wanted my body to look like. If I'd only followed those accounts, I might have found my outlines wanting. I might have pined for a smooth swimmer's triangle of a body. I might have felt even more enmity vis-à-vis my breasts than I did at the time. (The day I found out I was pregnant, I was excited for two reasons, the second of which was that I'd made a decision to delay relieving myself permanently of breasts until I'd had and nursed a kid—pregnancy lit the gas lamp at the end of that particular tunnel.) I know that many masculine-of-centre people have bodies like mine; I know it, but I sometimes can't help but feel that the shape of my body betrays me to onlookers.

Our culture is currently into bodies like Kim Kardashian's. Into them until they cross a line, into them until the same tendencies that allow for curves lead to monstrous—too big, too fat, too complicated—pregnancies. My own body has felt monstrous since it began to fit nowhere, exactly. The monstrousness of pregnancy came as no great shock or surprise; I knew to seek out writing and drawings by others who'd experienced pregnancies in bodies like mine. I understood not to take personally the aesthetic directions of the clothing at the maternity store. The two little lines on the stick showed up nearly two decades after I'd continually failed at thinness and femininity and girlhood, and I'd long before set those things aside and decided to accept myself for who I was.

I'VE BEEN GENDER NON-CONFORMING SINCE I WAS A KID. This so deeply disappointed one of my parents that it was part of the reason I had to learn to live without her love.

I always felt a bit like a boy, but not really like a boy. I always had crushes on boys, even as I found most of them wanting. I started googling "straight butch" as soon as I hit university and met more queer friends. Later, thanks to Tumblr, I came across the term "non-binary," and it clicked into place like an overall buckle over its button. By the time I met my partner, Will, I'd learned to negotiate relationship-related gender issues one by one: to seek out other soft, masculine people who'd want what I wanted—a balance where we were both close to the middle of the teeter-totter. But I was scared, even with Will, when I decided to tell him that I wouldn't always have breasts. "Fwwssht," I said, curling my hand up and away.

"How do you see me?" I asked him another time. He said he saw me like I'd once described the way I saw myself: as a person, first and foremost. I knew this was a privilege the rest of the world wouldn't afford me, just as it does not afford others, but I was relieved and full of gratitude to have it in my own home, in my own relationship.

WHEN WILL AND I GOT MARRIED, we wrote gender-neutral vows and both wore suits. We explained to our families that I wouldn't be going by bride, or wife—we'd be sticking with partner. We had a small, casual wedding three months after deciding to get married, and it all, language-wise, went fine enough.

Two and a half years later, when I got pregnant, I was reminded of my family's initial reaction when I told them Will and I were getting married: they'd never expected me to. Although no one had ever really verbalized that they'd seen my gender non-conformity, it was clear that they had seen it. They'd seen it and read it as a rejection of everything they associated with heteronormative gender roles. Whereas the wedding was a blip on the timeline of life, pregnancy and parenthood were much larger commitments—much larger commitments that my family, like perhaps a lot of people, see as the next in a row of conventionally heteronormative choices.

I'd been thinking of raising a kid in the context of my partnership with Will, the two of us sharing parenting and working as we share everything else. To the world outside my relationship, though, being the gestational parent who was coupled with a cis male partner immediately reinscribed womanhood and motherhood on me—it immediately reinscribed a gender, and a gender role, no one who really knew me well would ever have assumed prior.

Is this a problem of body, or language? I wondered.

I FIRST BROACHED THE "I'M NOT MOM" CONVERSATION with my brother and dad while visiting them, right after Will and I told them I was pregnant. We were sitting in a restaurant booth in a town at the tip of the Bruce Peninsula in Ontario, I was irritably hungry, and I'd just ordered nachos.

My brother, close in age and relationship but far away in life experience, wore a look of mild confusion.

"But you call me Dad, and that's gendered," my dad said.

And so it was, at thirty-two, I began to experience the raft of questions and comments and concerns one receives when one comes out. ("Not everyone will understand as well as me," "You know this is going to make things harder for you?" etc.)

As I floated ideas about what I might prefer to be called as an alternative to Mom or Dad—Zaza, Omma, Momo—my well-meaning family shot each and every one down.

Every time I felt I made headway, we backslid. I tried to remember to feel lucky to have family who loved us, family who wanted to try to understand, but the power of the pregnancy-female-mother connection was strong enough to efface all their efforts.

At my lowest points, hormonal and physically exhausted, I felt myself wilt like an unwatered, thirsty plant. I gave up trying to find an alternative. The truth is, I'm not an early adopter. If I could have, I would've given in, melted myself down, reformed as Mother. But I can't do that, either. So I decided I'd simply be the kid's parent. Instead of asking them to call me Mom or Dad, Zaza or Omma or Momo, I'd ask them to call me by my first name. I'd ask the kid; I'd ask my family. I'd ask and hope they'd listen.

BY NINETEEN WEEKS, I'D FELT THE FETUS FLUTTER A COUPLE TIMES: once when I was leaning a little too hard against the kitchen counter doing dishes; another time when I was lifting a heavy box of bike parts up onto a shelf at a bike co-op where I'd started volunteering. But mostly I felt nothing, and it worried me. When I was first pregnant, I researched rates of miscarriage by the age of the gestational parent, and the statistics were not extraordinarily comforting. I wrote in a poem that the world had been lying—there *was* such a thing as a "little bit pregnant." I began to talk about being pregnant before conventional wisdom says you're supposed to, and Will and I toured the neighbourhood thrift stores, buying and washing onesies and sweaters with creature themes. The anxiety passed after the first Doppler-amplified heartbeat, the first ultrasound. But it came back: statistically unlikely but still possible, something could have gone wrong in the second, or even the third, trimester. I could have the belly and then I could have a child, or I could have the belly and then it could deflate before any of the strangers I passed in the street even realized I was plump with child.

I did not feel dysphoric in my pregnant body. I felt different anxieties—about loss and death, primarily—but I did not feel dysphoric in my body. I felt dysphoric in the *language used* to talk about my body, my pregnant body.

BY TWENTY-TWO WEEKS, I needed but refused to buy a larger bra, hoping that, like goldfish, my breasts would only grow to the size of the bowl they were given.

By thirty weeks, I had both insomnia and some new tactics for approaching well-meaning loved ones who kept referring to me as Mom and Momma. My dad had taken to talking about my pregnancy by underscoring that he was looking forward to being a grandparent, not a grandfather; baffled and annoyed, I told him that what I would appreciate more was if he could expend some of that energy telling his friends, and underscoring to our family, my wishes when it came to names and terms and roles. "He's trying," Will said.

I decided that when we sent thank-you cards—our families and friends were so kind and supportive in so many ways, mailing notes and gifts as the due date approached—we could introduce the baby's name and reinforce the parent terms we'd use all at once.

Outside of the heavily gendered French-language health care system (where it was difficult enough, mentally, to understand directives in my second language), I began to gently employ a script correcting a friend, family member, or stranger's use of Mom. I started buying picture books that displayed a variety of different family structures, so that, I hoped, my own home would continue to be a place where I could more easily and without friction be myself. I'd become practised at the art of doing a simultaneous rewrite, in my head, of all the pregnancy literature so that it included me. If I needed to, I vowed to write and draw the books myself.

ALTHOUGH I'VE NEVER KNOCKED OVER MARGIE VII, Will's prize *Dracaena marginata*, our cat has felled her twice. Margie's pot bears a series of cracks and fissures; part of it has been reinforced with folded tinfoil. Every time the cat knocks over one of Will's plants—he deeply loves the cat; he deeply loves the plants—he gets mad at the cat. Then he superglues the pot back together; lovingly replants Margie, or Phil, or whoever else has been affected; sweeps up the debris; and forgives the cat. Similarly, I could wish for a simple wholeness that betrays no cracks or fissures, but I will be better served by learning to pick myself up and heal as many times as necessary.

jane

JANE IS TWENTY-NINE AND BISEXUAL. She grew up in Scarborough, Ontario, in a neighbourhood called Agincourt. It's where serial killer Bruce McArthur was Santa Claus at the mall every Christmas.

Scarborough in the nineties was diverse, and pretty immigrant-heavy. A lot of first-generation parents were coming to Canada and raising their second-generation kids there. Jane's neighbourhood started off pretty white, and then progressively became more Chinese. Jane's family had immigrated from Hong Kong, and she was born in Canada.

Where Jane first went to school, it was mostly a blend of Cantonese people and white people, second- and third-generation kids with parents from Eastern Europe. So you would consider them white, but they're still, in Canada, "ethnic." After grade four, Jane transferred to a school in the southeast end of Scarborough, where she was in a gifted program. The regular student population was mostly first- and second-generation kids from India, Sri Lanka, and Pakistan, and the gifted students were generally white, Cantonese, and Indian students.

There weren't a lot of girls in her gifted cohort, and it felt like a bit of a bubble experiment. She was close with her female friends, but everyone in the group was very close. Everyone was touchy-feely. So she didn't really clue into the fact that she was bisexual. It basically just felt like she was part of a weird group of weird children.

At school, hugging was okay, socially, as long as you didn't cross a certain line. Kissing would not have been cool. And it wasn't permissive emotionally, either. They were close, but there was a boundary that wasn't to be crossed.

Jane's high school was medium-sized—1,400 or 1,600 kids. There was a Gay–Straight Alliance, but it was not cool. No one was in it. They made fun of it: if you needed a club, you could always join the GSA so you could put it on your university application. But Jane's school did have trans kids—there were two. There were trans kids before there were queer kids. No one knew exactly how to act around the trans kids. It's not that they were malicious or mean. The kids were like, "Okay, so we don't deadname you?" The teachers were like, "Okay, so, what do we do about the bathrooms?" Same-sex marriage was legalized during the period Jane was in high school.

Jane was never transphobic or homophobic. She didn't have to go through any self-hate. But growing up, she didn't really notice other queer people. It felt like Ellen DeGeneres was the only example she'd ever seen. One of her teachers was part of a lesbian couple; she was with someone who'd previously graduated from their high school and taught somewhere else. Before Jane figured out they were a couple, she asked another teacher why they drove to work together. Jane said, "Oh, they must live close," and the teacher said, "Yes, they share a house." Years later, Jane's friend saw the couple at Pride. Jane was like, "That teacher didn't tell me they were sharing their lives together. They just told me they were sharing their house. What the fuck?"

Jane did not come out in high school. Her graduating class of gifted kids had maybe forty or fifty-five students, and maybe twenty percent of those students were girls. She had a crush on a girl, but all the guys had a crush on that girl, so they'd be like, "Jane's just being one of the bros." She didn't realize it at the time, but she was really depressed. Her depression superseded any exploration of her sexuality.

Around her friends in high school, there was an understanding that their parents had traditional thinking and mindsets, but that was only one way of thinking. When Jane got to university, she was exposed to a much wider variety of opinions. She realized that her parents' views weren't necessarily right, and that she didn't have to agree with them on everything. She's not out to her parents.

With her dad, it could go one of two ways. Either he'd be very mad about it, or he'd make an exception, and it would be okay. She's never sure where he's going to land, because he's kind of like Trump, in the sense that he'll say one thing, and then he'll forget he said it and say, "Oh, I didn't say that. Why are you putting words in my mouth?"

Jane used to keep a set of quotes that he said about gay people, because her psychiatrist asked her at one point. He hates gay people, and then he's okay with gay people, but then he hates gay people, and he hates trans people. It could go either way.

Her mom probably wouldn't understand. It took her a while to understand that Jane's clinical depression actually required a therapist. She'll seem to get it for a while, and be accepting, but she also downplays things. Jane thinks it's part cultural, but there's also something else going on. And Jane doesn't want to come out to her grandparents. They're fairly liberal but very old. She doesn't want to give them a literal heart attack.

Also, it's been a while since Jane was in a relationship that felt like it was worth talking about with her family. She's not going to rock the boat if she doesn't have to. If she did end up in a relationship with a woman, she knows she'd eventually have to bring it up with her parents, or risk a breakup with the person she was dating. She can't see that not ending a relationship.

Jane thinks that millennials did grow up in a generation of change for queer issues, but when you layer race into it, it gets more complicated. It can be a cultural thing as well as a generational thing. When Jane thinks about her neighbourhood, and the people she grew up with there, it feels like everyone is mysteriously straight. All the Asians are mysteriously straight. It's more the white kids from her gifted program that came out—later.

It's hard being a second-generation person, when there are a lot of cultural markers attached to your identity. Aside from dealing with her parents, things seem more complicated for her than they might be for a white queer person. When she goes on dating apps, for example, it's not that reassuring, because almost everybody is white. They all look the same: white, with the sides of their heads shaved. She doesn't see a lot of representation, so it's difficult to picture herself belonging on the app. Online dating is just generally depressing because she doesn't get any matches.

She feels like an Asian dude trying to date, like how OkCupid noticed that Asian dudes got the least messages. It can feel bleak. It's not necessarily that Jane is looking to date another Asian woman—though there are cultural differences she has to work with if she dates a white woman, like, "Oh, you don't know what Lao Gan Ma sauce is"—but rather that it would be reassuring to see other Asian women like her. And then one of the apps she was on only served her other Asian women, which also seemed kind of racist. Even when she dates guys, she feels a bit second-rate, in that she isn't a skinny Chinese girl who has long beautiful hair and perfectly manicured nails. She could get a manicure, but that's not going to make her look like a waif. She's not going to look like Constance Wu.

For Jane, the question of whether she feels like she had to leave Scarborough in order to be herself, to be comfortable with her sexuality, is difficult to answer. It's the wrong question. Jane felt like she had to go somewhere else because, if not, she was probably going to have a mental breakdown. All she ended up proving to herself, though, was that the location doesn't matter. She was headed for another depressive episode anyway. And she was ultimately too sad to have the opportunity to question what it even meant to be herself.

jamie

JAMIE IS A TRANS MAN WHO LIVES IN HAMILTON, ONTARIO, which is where he grew up. He's a dad to four kids. He never thought he'd have one kid, never mind four. It's the best thing life has had to offer so far, but it's also impossible to get anything done.

Jamie was born in 1984. He's an only child, and he always wanted a big family. He wanted people to love. Jamie had a pretty close relationship with his parents growing up, and he still does. But he hated being an only child. It felt kind of lonely. Sometimes he still feels lonely.

He grew up in a small apartment in the west end of Hamilton with his mom and dad on a quiet street with lots of young families. He spent most of his time playing road hockey with all the boys in the neighbourhood. He was what people called a tomboy.

It was more difficult at school because he went to a Catholic school and had the social norms for gender roles shoved down his throat. But that didn't stop him. He played foot hockey with the boys at recess and laughed at the girls when they cried, which he now feels a little bad about.

It wasn't until Jamie was older that he started to feel ashamed or bothered about being different. He just didn't relate to being a girl. The first time Jamie told his mom he was a boy was when he was three. Jamie only knows that he told his mom that he was a boy at three because she told him about it when he came out to her as trans. Jamie said, "Well, what the fuck, Mom." (He's kidding. It made him feel validated.)

His class photos growing up paint a picture of his life. His mom would dress him up and do his hair, and he would get to school and dunk his hair in the sink and soak it to get the style out. Bows and braids. Every year. On special occasions his mom would make him wear dresses, but mostly he got to wear what he wanted. He remembers having tantrums on the special occasions. His mom would say, "Too bad, you're a girl." She didn't know any different.

His parents used to have to buy him a new hat to get the old one off his head. He wore hockey everything. Coats, hats. Growing up, hockey was the place where Jamie didn't feel limited by gender expectations. On the ice, he was just doing what he loved. He didn't start playing until he was ten, because at first his dad said girls don't play, and he had to beg and beg.

He played boys' hockey as a goalie for one season. His dad thought being a goalie would be better because he was a girl. It didn't last long, though. He wanted to skate. He played on two teams the next year—one boys, one girls—and then the third year he played girls rep hockey. As he got older, it was harder to play boys' hockey because he was not allowed in the change room.

The girls' team was easier because no matter how well he played with the boys, or how much better than them he was, he was always just "the girl." And the group of people he met playing girls hockey ended up being the most solid friends he ever made, still to this day.

Meeting accepting people at hockey allowed Jamie to start dating women. But it made it a bit harder to come out as trans. He was nineteen when he realized he was probably trans. He met his first trans guy and he instantly made the connection to his own feelings and experiences. But the guy was a bit of a disaster, did too many drugs, and lived a life that felt kind of dysfunctional. And then Jamie met the love of his life, and she was a lesbian. Jamie wasn't sure if he could tell her how he felt. He wasn't sure she'd accept him. Then they had kids. Jamie had a hard time deciding to transition. He had a lot to lose. He was happy on one level—his wife and his kids were his life. But if he came out, would she stay with him? Would he be destroying his kids' lives? It was heavy. He stopped caring about himself and became Super Parent and got depressed and gained a lot of weight.

Jamie's son is why he had the courage to be true to himself. Jamie's son is his hero. Jamie had told him not to be a follower, to be himself no matter what people thought—yet, his son said, Jamie wasn't following his own advice. Jamie's son was sixteen at the time. He had a trans friend in high school, and he intuited that Jamie was trans. Jamie and his son are really close.

Jamie's wife did stand by him. It was hard for her, too, because it did change everything she thought she knew about herself. She'd had an inkling about Jamie's gender, but she didn't want to tell him how she felt in case she was wrong.

The next person Jamie talked to was his doctor. He and his wife had had a lot of talks with her when they were trying to conceive. It just so happens that Jamie's doctor is the trans care doctor for all of Hamilton. When Jamie came out to her, she gave Jamie a "Well, it's about time" response. They'd talked previously about Jamie's thoughts on carrying a baby. Jamie was like, "Never!"

Jamie started his transition at home. His kids called him Dad for a bit before he thought about work or hormones. As soon as his daughter said "Daddy" the first time, he melted. It was perfect. His kids were okay, so he was okay. He had that first conversation with his son about five years ago, and then his kids started calling him "dad" about four years ago. Prior to that, he read and read and read, articles and stories and studies. But he still felt a bit scared. He had a job he loved, and he wanted to retire with that job. He wasn't sure if coming out would fuck with that. How would he feed his kids? His daughter was sick, too. It just didn't feel like the right time to put himself first. His kids came first.

Eventually, though, he realized he was sick of feeling like crap. Coming out was tough, but it made his family stronger. He started testosterone, and it was exhilarating. Within weeks, his voice started to change. He made weekly recordings to document it. He thought maybe he'd sound like his dad, but he sounds like his mom's brother.

And then he had to talk to his boss. Thankfully, his boss and his company were great. Jamie runs a paint store. It's a good gig. He keeps getting promoted.

Jamie's parents struggled a bit at first with not understanding his gender, and there are still some things they disagree on. Misgendering him was the biggest battle. It was hard for them. They try their best.

It was also difficult in the context of hockey and other parts of Jamie's life. Jamie played hockey until about six years ago. He stopped before he transitioned, when it was already becoming hard. The last year he played women's hockey, Jamie stopped showing up sometimes because he started finding it harder to deal with showering and trying to be something he wasn't. His attendance was too spotty and the coach asked him not to play the next year. Jamie wasn't being reliable, but he also didn't tell them why. Now that he no longer gets misgendered, and he's had top surgery, no one would know, so he could start playing hockey with guys again. He plans to soon.

When Jamie got top surgery, he thought he'd wake up feeling so happy, but it wasn't exactly like that because of the bandages. After a week he got to actually see himself for the first time. He came home and went upstairs and sobbed. Every bit of emotion he'd stressed about came flowing out. He could go swimming. He could play hockey again. He could wear a tank top without a binder. He'd never been so happy. His wife, his kids, his family, they see his joy. It was life-altering.

Jamie thinks his next surgery will be hard for him. He no longer looks like a woman even slightly, and he'll have to go sit in a waiting room to get a hysterectomy with a bunch of women and girls and wait for his name to be called. It's a lot.

Jamie understands wanting to leave the place where you grew up. It might have been easier for him to start fresh. Running into people can be awkward. But what would that teach his kids? He chose to cope. Jamie was a parent early. His daughter was born when he was twenty-one. His wife is older and came into the relationship with a son, who was six. They've been together for about fifteen years and married for more than ten. When their kids got older, they started over again and had more. They now have a four-year-old and a two-year-old as well.

When Jamie thinks about being trans and having had the world change so much as he grew up and transitioned and had kids of his own, it's nice to see his kids face fewer struggles, but it does feel bittersweet for him. Then again, if his life had been different and he'd transitioned earlier, he probably wouldn't have met his wife and had his kids, and they're his lights, the lights of his life.

5

DEATH AND BIRTH

IT'S THE MOST NORMAL THING IN THE WORLD to be born and the most normal
thing to die. When Sinclair was born, I was holding onto consciousness
as if my mind were two sets of fingers gripping a narrow ledge. I was
supposed to have a planned C-section. Sinclair was breech and when I
researched the risks, it seemed like I would incur more and she would
incur fewer if she was born that way. We'd tried a procedure to turn her;
an obstetrician at the hospital had pressed her hands to my stomach and
gotten Sinclair halfway before Sinclair ducked and wouldn't keep turning.
The obstetrician turned her back to breech.

I had an epidural before the C-section, and I reacted poorly to the
anaesthetic. I was being prepped for surgery and Will wasn't yet in the
room. My blood pressure dropped and Sinclair's heart rate dropped and
the edges of the room went blurry and the doctors and nurses began
to move very quickly. A nurse knelt by my ear and described what was

happening. Her voice was quiet and reassuring. I felt the scalpel at my stomach as if the blade were a memory instead of a current event. Everything was happening very fast and very slow, very close and very far away.

When Sinclair emerged and let out a wail, I began to cry as if it was the first time I'd ever cried, as if tears were part of the viscera of birth. Two nurses asked me if I was okay. Was I okay? "I'm fine," I said, sobbing. "I'm fine. Just overwhelmed."

Will was ushered in, brought to Sinclair, just as they were about to do her Apgar test, which would measure her breathing, heart rate, muscle tone, and colour. The blue hadn't yet faded from her skin. And then Will sat behind me to the left, where the nurse had been sitting, and someone, maybe my OB/GYN, put Sinclair on my chest. She was curled up like a little frog and seemed impossibly small. As my OB stitched me up, he joked with the nurses in French. "That was quick," someone must have said to him. "Under four minutes," he responded. "Three and a half."

EARLIER IN THE PREGNANCY, Will and I were sitting in a corridor at Montreal's CHU Sainte-Justine, waiting to take a gestational diabetes test, when a pregnant woman collapsed. The hallway was full of pregnant women, sitting in a row of chairs lined up against the wall, all at various stages of the hour-long test. Nurses rushed to help the woman who'd collapsed. They helped her into a small room off the hallway; she was murmuring and moaning. Five minutes later, the hospital called a code blue, meaning a critical medical emergency, like cardiac or respiratory arrest: our floor, our block, the room number where the nurses had rushed the woman. I noted the nearest exit stairwell—down the white-tiled hallway, a short 200-metre dash—just as a nurse called my name to start the test. I looked at Will, who nodded in the direction of the nurse's station with his chin, and I reluctantly let him walk me down the hallway. We passed a cluster of nurses and residents gathered outside the woman's room. If I believed in God, I would have prayed for her (and for myself). As it was, all I could do was take a few deep breaths to calm my nerves.

Maternal mortality rates are relatively low in Canada, around 9 for every 100,000 deliveries. Before I got pregnant, I thought the deaths of gestational parents existed solely in the context of childbirth, the Gothic and tragic kind you see depicted in books and on television—Lady Sybil on Downton Abbey, Oliver's mother in Oliver Twist, Cathy's mother in Wuthering Heights. In reality, mortality rates include deaths during pregnancy, childbirth, and up to forty-two days after childbirth. Rates are tied to direct and indirect factors, everything from the age of the gestational parent to circulatory disorders and hypertension to access to education and regular medical care. Less discussed: a more recent meta-study discovered that one in nineteen deaths of gestational parents in Ontario between 1994 and 2008 resulted from suicide.

At twenty-six weeks pregnant, I thought about dying several times a day. Thirty-two years old and in good health, I had none of the physical risk factors associated with death before, during, or after childbirth. I had access to high-quality medical care; through our local community centre, Will and I went to a free prenatal education class where we learned about labour, which I wouldn't experience, and breastfeeding and caring for a newborn, which I would.

I was worried that I would die, and that Sinclair wouldn't make it to birth. When I learned I was pregnant, it felt tentative, like something that could be taken away at any time. I tried not to, but I made bargains in my head: if we get to twelve weeks, the pregnancy will last; if we get to thirty-five, she'll be born safe. Another bargain: once the fetus reached viability, Will promised to wear a helmet while he rode his bike.

My doctor's appointments proceeded well. I was physically fine. By my second trimester, though, I'd started to experience a blue hour. Mid-afternoon, I cried until I was heaving. One day, the sight of my cat curled up on my bed reminded me of a fox-fur stole, and I pictured her little body, evacuated of life, and burst into tears. Another day, when I was about to go for a bike ride, I was overcome with memories of every car accident I'd ever been in or witnessed. My usual anxiety about death had been ratcheted up past the boundary of the volume knob. I told myself that I was lucky and that it was nothing but a type of selfish empathy to keep thinking about the woman who collapsed during her gestational diabetes test. I thought about accessing psychiatric care through the hospital but dismissed the idea as soon as the peak of each wave passed. I didn't want to sponge up resources that could be better used for someone else, I didn't want to be unwell, and on a very basic level I thought—because I'd previously attempted to treat it—that there was no real cure for my anxiety about mortality. In retrospect, I was also so worried about developing post-partum depression, or, worse to me, postpartum mania, that I neglected to notice that I'd developed a type of antenatal depression I probably should have sought help for.

Instead, I made more bargains. After reading the study about suicide and maternal mortality, I promised myself I'd go to the doctor if obsessively fearing death began to feel like standing on a suspension bridge and experiencing a downwards visual tug towards the chasm. Sinclair reached twelve weeks, and then thirty-five. I had some late-term pregnancy complications and couldn't understand why we weren't just yanking her out. She was small and breech, and I began to itch all over, as if I'd become allergic to being pregnant. The longer we could wait, the better, the doctors said, but I didn't fully trust them.

After she was born, for no good reason, Will and I both were worried that maybe she'd die in the night if we didn't watch her closely enough. She was strong. She was bright and alert. She drank so much milk. Still, Will and I stayed up late listening to her ragged breathing. We'd learned all about how newborns adapt to life outside the womb—they pause between breaths, they can make what sound like gurgling or choking noises, they breathe very rapidly, not very evenly—but in practice it was very hard to tell what was terrifyingly normal and what constituted a sign that she needed to be whisked off to urgent care. We worried, yet we continued to be lucky. Sinclair got to six months and then a year old, officially out of SIDS territory. And then it became clear that all the survival goals I'd set—twelve weeks gestation, thirty-five, birth, six months, a year—though statistically meaningful, would never bring me the relief I was seeking. I would need to accept a different kind of relief, or accept that relief would never come.

I AM NOW THIRTY-FIVE AND SINCLAIR IS TWO YEARS OLD. My dad is in his early sixties and so is Will's mom; Will's dad has reached his seventies. Sinclair even has two and half living sets of great-grandparents. When I was her age, I had one set. Most of my grandparents lived through the Second World War, and my maternal granddad was an airplane mechanic, stationed on the west coast of Africa. None of them lived in prewar Canada, but they all lived in postwar Canada; most came from England and one, later, from Jamaica. Together, linked as a family, our lifespans cover a lot of history; I like to think about these links, and to picture my grandparents at Sinclair's age. But Sinclair's arrival also reminds me how temporary this is: eventually, she will be older and my grandparents will no longer be alive. I won't get to have them all, together, for as long as I'd like.

Will and I had Sinclair at the right time for our lives, but I wish the numbers marking our ages were smaller. If the numbers were smaller, then statistically, we'd have more time with her. I am gripped by this counting-focused anxiety, even as I know that life isn't statistics: my time could end now, or next week.

SEVERAL YEARS AGO, people in North America began to write more about death. About how the rituals of death here have been sanitized, about how we're too far from it, how we'd have a healthier relationship with it if we cultivated a bodily closeness. Doulas helped people through the liminal state between womb and outside world, so death doulas emerged in the popular consciousness, guiding the dying and their families through the process of moving from existence to non-existence.

But distance from death is a first-world problem, and one that isn't even experienced by everyone in the first world. Mortality rates vary fairly significantly by race, economic status, and gender identity. Between 2016 and 2019, the opioid crisis killed over 14,700 people in Canada—that number has been climbing year after year, and thousands more people would have died if not for the administration of naloxone. Many communities, often Indigenous communities, don't have clean, potable water; many more, sometimes overlapping, are affected by the kind of environmental racism that makes it unsafe to breathe, to swim, to live. As a result of this and many other long-term and continuing state policies, the lifespans of

Indigenous Peoples in Canada are fifteen years shorter than the average. Trans people, in particular trans women, in particular trans women of colour, also don't generally have to think abstractly about how close death is or could be: the current US average lifespan for a trans woman of colour is thirty-five years, a number I can quote without googling.

Still, middle-class people in cities and suburbs keep having the same conversation about whether photos of dead people, often drowned, often refugees, should be shared on social media. The idea is that to allow death to be proximate and visible is to increase empathy, to make death, and in particular this kind of death, real for those of us who lead safe lives, those of us who can turn on the tap and drink the water that comes out.

I am against showing the photos. The dead were living, breathing humans with interior lives as full and rich as mine. I don't need to see photos to "humanize" them or the circumstances that war and conflict and politics forced them into. They are already human. All they were trying to do was live. When I am falling asleep, if I haven't managed to avoid seeing the pictures, I see the pictures. They've been added to the carousel of images I would like to wipe clean, a carousel that haunts me. Also on the carousel are hypothetical images of Sinclair: potential violence, illness. I try to banish the images. I stay up late picturing the images and banishing them. I read several times about how to save tomato seeds, pea seeds, basil, how to coax a new plant from the life the parent plant has given, as the images recur. I feel sorry, and who I want to apologize to is the dead, who have been desecrated. I'm not sure why we need to view their lifeless bodies in order to push the state to be responsible for killing fewer people. I'm not sure why we—the "we" many people think about every four years at the ballot box, the "we" some of us are more complicit with than others—need to be responsible for killing so many people, when any other alternative seems preferable.

When I interrogate the way I feel about life and death, I think about how life is a cycle that runs through matter. I want everyone to live forever, but that is not the way life works. When I interrogate the way I feel about life and death, I wish I could think less about death while I am still living.

IN TOM SCOCCA'S ARTICLE "Your Real Biological Clock Is You're Going to Die," he plays the same game of sliding numbers that I've been playing since I was a kid and began to obsessively subtract my family members' ages from Canada's average lifespans for men and women. ("How old are you?" I'd ask my nana again and again, as she demurred. "What year were you born?") "Everyone who was forty-seven years old when my father was born is now dead," Scocca writes. "All of them. That entire group of middle-aged people, who made up the adult world when my father was a child, is gone." The essay is a meditation on the ways our culture thinks of time as something one gains through age, rather than something that slowly ticks away. Basically: the longer you skateboard, the more you push off parenthood, the longer you think you're young. For Scocca, what made reality click into place—that's not how time or age works *at all*—was the reality of having a kid. "If you intend to have children, but you don't intend to have them just yet, you are not banking extra years as a person who is still too young to have children," he writes. "You are subtracting years from the time you will share the world with your children."

The largest part of me identifies with Scocca's new-found fixation on mortality, generations, kids, parents, grandparents, life; a smaller part of me doesn't, because I've never thought of time the other way. Not for the same reason that most trans women and people assigned female at birth probably wouldn't—the overwhelming message to women and girls is that your worth is tied to beauty and fertility, and both of those things have a looming expiry date—but because this numbers game has been my game forever, and it seems naive to me that Scocca got to it so late.

It might just be heterosexual cis white men, in particular WASP-y ones, who get to skateboard nonchalantly into their mid-forties. The averages for some of us lengthen, whereas others bear the weight of earlier death—the ultimate expression of how our society is uneven, inequitable, unequal, unfair. The libertarian response to this might be that life is not fair, and it is stupid to expect fairness, but the truth is that some of the people who die young do so in order that we might grow old. The water company drains an aquifer to send bottles to Arizona; twenty minutes down the road, the residents of an Indigenous community have no clean drinking water. I am not saying that Tom Scocca should feel bad that the weight of time hit him a decade later than many trans women die, but I am saying that all of us who have a reasonable assumption of becoming octogenarians should not literally be taking life from others in order to get there.

WHEN SINCLAIR WAS BORN, Justin Trudeau was prime minister. When I was born, his father, Pierre, had just stepped down. When my dad was born, Louis St. Laurent was just about to be replaced by John Diefenbaker. When my grandmother was born, William Lyon Mackenzie King—the Presbyterian spiritualist who communed with the dead via mediums and Ouija boards—was in power. I learned about the October Crisis and the Quiet Revolution in school as if they were a chapter that had ended several chapters back, not realizing the same long-serving prime minister who was in power around the time I was born had been in charge for most of it. The longer I am alive, the closer history seems—and the more it becomes clear that the people I love and care about lived through eras I used to consider the distant and undisturbable past. Put another way: it was when I started being able to reliably answer Trivial Pursuit questions that I knew I was fucked.

When I was pregnant and crying every day at three p.m., I sobbed uncontrollably like I used to when we'd leave my maternal grandparents' house in Florida to go back north. Part of me thought that if I held onto my grandparents tight enough, I'd never have to let them go. When I cried while pregnant, the sorrow was the same: my grandfather had died, and my nana, siding with my estranged mother, no longer wanted to speak to me. Why was the sorrow the same before I knew what the loss felt like, when I was just anticipating it? Why did it still feel the same after I did?

Every day I live with the discomfort that I might die today, that I will die someday, that everyone I care about will die, probably my grandparents first—it's supposed to start like that and then go on down the line, because that's how it works when you are lucky and privileged, and you should be grateful for it. I know now that the idea that Sinclair would get to a safe point—past miscarriage, past SIDS—was fantastical. The days ticking forward are teaching me that it's fantastical. New worries have replaced the old ones.

I have always wanted something that did not add up on an abacus, or anywhere else. At the same time as I want to live forever, and I want the people I care about to live forever, I also want there to be space and time for everyone to live forever, not just everyone wealthy and white.

I need Sinclair to be able to live forever even more than I want to live forever myself. (I even regularly tell my cat that she needs to live to be the oldest cat in the world, a Guinness World Record–holding cat.) Unlike Scocca, I have worried about mortality my whole life. Like Scocca, having a kid threw the normal progression of time, and what it would mean for me, and for her, into a terrifying new kind of relief. Even if I could quiet the part of my brain that imagines worst-case scenarios as if imagining them were the first step of a protective spell to banish them, I would still, impossibly, want us all to live forever.

erin

ERIN WAS BORN IN 1986. She grew up in a hamlet called Munster, in Ontario, a rural part of what has now been amalgamated into Ottawa. Munster was not really a town by itself. It felt like a subdivision that somebody took out into the middle of nowhere and left there. There was a Becker's convenience store for a while. There was an elementary school that went to grade five. A couple of rotating restaurants that were always going in and out of business. The high school was a couple of towns over. Erin grew up with a good group of kids, who all went to the same elementary school, had the same babysitters. It was a good place to be a kid but kind of a shitty place to be a teenager. Nothing to do and no place to go.

The apartment Erin lives in right now is maybe 300 square feet, but growing up, she lived in quite a large house. It was on a quarter-acre lot, and there was an in-ground pool in the backyard. Her dad always threatened to fill it in if she and her younger sister didn't help take care of it, which they never did. But they did swim in it a lot. It was very hot in Munster in the summertime.

Erin's house was a blocky, square thing with a two-car garage and four bedrooms. Her family didn't go into the living room unless they had company; it had a pink-velvet couch with matching swivelling chairs. Behind that were the kitchen and dining room. When Erin was a kid, the dining room had low-pile orange-brown carpet. Almost plaid, but not quite. To the right of the kitchen and dining room was a bathroom, and then the family room, which had blue high-pile carpet. Erin's room had royal blue carpet. The best carpet in the house. Very plush.

Erin's family eventually redecorated all the rooms, but hers was in the worst shape when they first moved in, when she was four, so she got to choose what it would look like. She chose blue with a rainbow wallpaper accent. A whole wall of rainbow. It stayed that way until she was eighteen and moved out.

When Erin was a teenager, her parents ripped out the kitchen and put in all new appliances and cupboards, a giant kitchen island that had a gas range in it, Italian tile all over the place. A lot of Erin's memories of that house, and of growing up, and of her dad specifically, are of cooking. Good times and bad times. She lost some friends in a car crash when she was a teenager. She went to school, and she came home at 3:30, and her dad was home from work, making ravioli. The whole kitchen was covered in ravioli. That's still what she does with her dad now, when she goes home. They cook things.

Erin spent a lot of time in her room, but when she moved out, she didn't really take anything with her. Just her books. She didn't have an awesome time in high school. She doesn't know anybody who did. She did a lot of hiding in her bedroom, not wanting to socialize, ever.

When she left Munster, her purpose was mostly just to go to university. Munster not being a town unto itself meant that it didn't have the same kind of small-town narrative you often hear, where people never leave, or never need to leave. She didn't feel stuck in Munster, or like she needed to make a permanent break. She always had access to her parents' cars.

Erin didn't have queer friends in high school. She went to a Catholic school, so that sort of thing was frowned upon. She didn't have any sense that bisexuality was a thing. She thought about it mostly in relation to this one fair-haired grade-twelve girl who she played soccer with for many, many years. Erin was like: Boys, but also Melanie. What's up with that?

Erin had a sense of wanting to be honest with herself. Within the framework of either/or, she wasn't sure what she would do if the answer was that she was a lesbian, or how that would manifest, or what would happen, or what anybody would say. It was very abstract. She wasn't dating or having sex in high school at all.

Going to Kingston for university felt like a chance to start over. Erin was stoked to get to school and join the newspaper. She finally met people who she could be actual friends with, to feel some kind of support and care from. It felt like a very safe break. Kingston was two hours from her house, and four generations of her family had gone to Queen's, so she could find her last name in various places on campus. Her great-grandfather was a dean at Queen's in the 1930s. She had the leather Queen's jacket with the crest on it. Ottawa was still her home base, and it was pretty easy to access when she wanted to. But two hours was enough distance that no one was going to drop in on her, or know about what she was doing every day.

It took a while for Erin to realize that she could be queer, or she could be bisexual, and that if she hadn't had it figured out by the time she was sixteen, that was fine, too. It took a lot of time for her to own her bisexuality, to come to terms with it and understand it and feel comfortable being more public about it. She had no frame of reference at all. She had no way to map herself onto those possible identities, to see if anything fit. Growing up with no queer role models was hard.

6

MILK AND TIME

IF I CLOSE MY EYES, I can picture the bathroom at work in great detail: a refill container of watermelon soap on the top of the vanity; white walls and doors smudged by touch in their high-traffic areas; a white-coated wire cart containing spare toilet paper rolls and a reusable bag full of clean hand towels. Inside the cabinet, relics of privacy: tampons, toothbrush, dental floss. The light switch is cockeyed, pointing northwest. The door-knob has a button lock, and I fear one day someone will walk in on me, sitting on the closed toilet seat, pumping. Sometimes voices bunch up outside the door, chatting in the public hallway, separated just barely from my private space. The bathroom light is connected to an overhead fan that rumbles as if it has croup; the bathroom fan obscures the noise of the pump's motor.

My pumping routine proceeds by muscle memory—unplug the mouse deterrent in the hallway, plug in the extension cord, tamp it down with my foot to close the bathroom door. Connect the pump's cord into the extension cord, connect the bottle heads to the bottles, connect the tubes to the bottles, turn on the power.

The first time I pump, I've just arrived at work. At the beginning of the week, I turn my phone face down and place it on the side of the sink. I focus on my breathing, to centre myself. I read somewhere that looking at a picture of one's infant while pumping can help increase milk production, so I conjure a recent memory. But by the end of the week—my daily commute having wrung me of willpower—I sit hunched over to keep the bottles in place as I scroll through Twitter and answer emails.

When I switched back to full-time, in-office work from freelancing, Sinclair was five months old—still exclusively drinking breast milk. The act of feeding her became routinized, measured in ounces. Keeping up my supply meant never missing a pumping session; it meant drinking 100 ounces of water a day. It meant nursing Sinclair three times a day, and pumping five times a day: 9 a.m., 11 a.m., 2:30 p.m., 4:30 p.m., 9 p.m. Whatever else I did, my day was given its rhythm through the act of expressing milk. Milk, milk milk milk milk milk.

MIRJAM GUESGEN, A FREELANCE SCIENCE JOURNALIST, wrote a feature about dairy farming in Canada for *Maisonneuve* in 2018, while I was editing for the magazine. Guesgen visited farms where the dairy cows didn't get to go outside very much at all—the most common situation in Canada—and others where the cows went out on a regular, if not daily, basis. My favourite moment in the piece comes when Guesgen is standing in a field with farmer Louis Fleurent, being investigated by "curious pink noses." The cows (and Guesgen and Fleurent) are outside during a light rain shower.

They like this, Fleurent says, and there will "be a little boost in how much milk the cows make today."

When French settlers brought cows to Canada in the seventeenth century, Guesgen writes, their enclosures were often huddled in against the settlers' homes. In the summertime, the cows grazed outside. In the winter, they remained mostly indoors, contributing their body heat as well as their milk to the family good.

Today, most humans live in urban centres, few of us own cows, and we've applied the laws of industry to milk production. As I learned— staying hydrated and paying careful attention to my diet—nutrition is a key determining factor in how many ounces (or litres) of milk you'll get. Cows are generally fed a combination of plants, like grass or hay or barley, and "concentrate," a mixture of carbohydrates, proteins, fats, minerals, and vitamins, generally by-products from other types of farming—canola meal, soy hulls, beet pulp, corn gluten. They drink between 80 and 180 litres of water per day.

Dairy cattle produced over 9.3 billion litres of milk in Canada in 2018– 2019; each cow produced an overwhelming annual average of 10,519 litres over the course of their year-long lactation cycle. But averages mask the underlying truth that the milk production of cows varies just as much as the milk production of humans. In 2016, a cow from Wisconsin named Gigi made the news for producing about 34,000 litres of milk over the course of her lactation cycle—triple the production of an average cow. Although she's in a category of her own, Gigi is also part of a trend: the average rate of milk production per US cow per year grew to 10,432 litres in 2017, up from 9,299 litres in 2008.

In the US, most cows go through three pregnancy and lactation cycles after first calving somewhere between two and three years of age, and then they are culled for food—the waning milk production of their fourth, fifth, or sixth lactation cycle means that it no longer makes economic sense to keep them around. (This wasn't always the case. As we've bred cows to produce more and more milk, their lifespans have decreased.) Cows who are low producers—say, twelve or fifteen litres per day instead of the average of thirty—are often culled earlier. As for their calves, they're usually separated a day or two after they enter the world; they're then fed milk (less than they'd take directly from their parent), or a milk substitute, and housed with their peers.

Like humans, cows who listen to music while they pump produce more milk. Several studies—including one from 1990 called "Moosic Is for Cows, Too"—have shown that slower-tempo music, like Beethoven's *Pastoral Symphony* (a particularly boring piece of music that also happens to score the flying horses segment of Disney's most soporific movie, *Fantasia*), decreases the cows' stress levels and encourages them to head to the milking machine. Their milk production is better when they are healthy, when they get to go outside, when they get to socialize with other cows on their own terms (cows have cows they like more, and cows they like less).

Dairy cattle loom large in the human imaginary—black-and-white Holsteins are one of the first animals we learn about as kids after dog, cat, bunny. Cows are their curious pink noses, and they are a key source of sustenance, and they are one of several figures in a farmer's economic ledger. They are a collective; they are also individuals with their own personalities, their own aches and pains and preferences. I thought about them a lot while I sat alone, drinking water and pumping.

IN MID-JUNE, just after we celebrate Sinclair's half birthday, my iPhone is on its way out. It sheds at least sixty-three percent of its battery while I am waiting for the bus, which is late—the highway is backed up behind 174 Street in Surrey. Eventually, the bus comes and I take it the forty or forty-five minutes to Surrey Central station, where I catch the Expo Line into Vancouver. The train gets stuck at Nanaimo. Every few minutes, SkyTrain control broadcasts a message: *Ladies and gentlemen. We have a problem train in the downtown area. We have staff on hand currently to remove the problem train, but there will be some short delays.* My phone is long dead and I am people watching on the packed train. Man in baseball cap with eyes closed. Child who earlier refused seat tugging at father's coat. Woman playing Candy Crush with the sound on.

When SkyTrain control says their staff is on hand to remove the problem train, I immediately picture a team of Thomas the Tank Engine figurines dismantling the train piece by piece, as if it is an overgrown snake in a sewer and there is no other way to solve the problem. Of course that can't be right—they are probably pushing or hauling it to a spur track—but the image persists.

Eventually, the train moves and I get to work only to realize that the pump's batteries are low. The pump wheezes along, more slowly than usual; I stare at the wall with my dead phone in my pocket, feeling as though the sapped batteries and the slow bus and the stuck train are all fine metaphors for how I feel commuting three hours a day while also pumping enough milk every day to ensure that our stockpile is growing instead of being depleted.

In late July, I get sick with a fever and go home early from work. I lie down to take a nap, and when I wake up, my face is swollen. The doctor at the walk-in clinic asks, "Your face doesn't always look like that?" It must be simultaneously a virus and an allergic reaction, she says, shrugging. I regret getting out of bed. It is my body saying, "No!" and then "No!" again, several more times, just in case. Will brings Sinclair upstairs and I feed her lying down side by side in bed. I feed her, but being sick means I have less milk, and a slower letdown, and Sinclair gets frustrated. I have a fever, and my milk has slowed down, right in the middle of a heat wave, when Sinclair is extra thirsty. She bites me because the milk isn't coming fast enough. She bites me and I cry, and the tears roll down my swollen face.

The fever passes, but the milk won't come back. There's enough for Sinclair when I'm with her but not when I pump. I read about how to increase my supply and the blogs are tailored to lactating parents who are at home with their babies. *Take a breastfeeding honeymoon*, they say. *Stay in bed all day with your baby and focus on feeding her!*

I learn that fenugreek and blessed thistle are galactagogues—they increase milk production. The blogs always mention that fenugreek should be a "last resort" when it comes to increasing milk—try a babymoon!—but they never spell out why. Increased risk of mastitis, I learn, eventually. On a weekend when I have several edits to complete and a lit mag to lay out, I also start taking fenugreek and blessed thistle. I am drinking almond milk, date, and oat smoothies with hemp seeds—all foods purported to help boost milk production. I am pumping for twenty minutes a session instead of my usual lazy five to seven. I am ordering

Mother's Milk tea and holding my selfhood back as I glean wisdom from the kinds of sources that claim your femininity will be strengthened if you spend time in a yurt. I am taking the bus and the train and pumping and taking the train and the bus, every day, every day, every day (people do this their whole lives!).

A body-seated memory crops up unbidden on the SkyTrain, between 22nd Street and Edmonds stations, where I pass, to the south, a cemetery and then a blue stucco house whose roof reads, ISLAM? READ QURAN. The memory is of a time when I was hauling a fifty-pound bag of potatoes from my best friend's dad's store to the Air Force Club, where my best friend's dad was drinking with my mom, where a friend of theirs was running a catering company. Hauling the potatoes as if they were the torso of an incapacitated man. As soon as the memory comes, I realize I don't want to remember it. It recurs at regular intervals. It's a memory I've put in a poem, a memory that reminds me that my mother once asked me to apologize to a man who'd groped me because I must have misunderstood why his hand crept down my back, crept down to the small of my back; she asked me to apologize because I said no or stop or go away. A protective bad memory, one that reminds me to enforce my physical boundaries and to avoid my mother. But I haven't spoken to my mother in years. The threat has passed; I left through an alternative exit to avoid saying sorry and I will keep leaving through alternative exits to avoid ever saying sorry.

In August I am trying as hard as I can. I have become a person with a 6:30 a.m. vitamin alarm. By the end of August my milk is running again, some days more plentifully than others. We are three-quarters of the way to one year. Sinclair has started to eat solid food: cereal, bananas, noodles with sauce, steamed yams. We are staying at a friend's home in Vancouver and Sinclair is upstairs asleep in what we refer to as her nap tent, and I've asked half my brain to think about milk and the other half to think about the cover for a poetry book. I am relieved that my milk came back. I am thinking about how much everybody loves Sinclair. I am hoping that Sinclair always loves herself as much as everybody loves her right now.

WHILE "FED IS BEST" has somewhat supplanted "breast is best"—itself a response to the commodification of baby feeding, during a time when families were being encouraged to use formula and told that it was better than breast milk—the recommended best practice for feeding infants is still breast milk. Posters in the waiting rooms of the hospitals and the pediatrician's offices and at the OB/GYN underscore this message; it feels, at times, like the public health message is designed to "educate" mothers who use formula, as if the most important thing standing between them and making the best choice is ignorance and not a complex mix of economic factors, time constraints, and other pressures.

When I worked at Adbusters, the publisher and editor-in-chief once remarked that women had ruined Western society by allowing television to raise their children. Though not all families with kids even include a mother, though a large percentage of American mothers don't have access to any maternity leave, though white mothers get to breastfeed at higher rates than Black mothers for a million and seven different reasons, though Canadian mothers who are poor generally can't afford to take maternity leave, though Canadian mothers who freelance don't generally qualify to take maternity leave, the "natural work" of raising and feeding and nurturing young children is still seen as being the purview of the mother, and when that work doesn't reach the superlative, it is considered the fault of the mother.

Though I am not a mother, I am the one who produces Sinclair's milk. As I am burning out on the SkyTrain, and pumping and pumping and pumping, I come across an article that suggests that not only is breast milk best, but that this milk should ideally come directly from nursing. I watch the first episode of a TV show where a breast milk pump is a prop for a thin white executive who has begrudgingly gone back to work, who leaks through her shirt while helping land a dairy company account. I have yet to see, on TV, a twenty-two-year-old at her retail job pumping in an overstock closet while her manager knocks on the door to remind her that her break ends in two minutes. I've yet to see a trans dad cycling across the city with an insulated cooler to pick up supplemental breast milk from someone he met through Facebook.

I've read everything I could get my hands on about milk, milk expression, infant nutrition, and infant wellness. In the absence of being able to always feed Sinclair directly, I've tried harder at pumping than I have tried at anything in my entire life. Will stays at home with Sinclair and he thaws the milk and Sinclair lays her head in the crook of his arm and he tilts the bottle up and she drinks the milk as fast as is humanly possible—and it's still not enough to be the best. She is fed. We are not the best because we are lower middle class and I am not a mother and the parent with the milk goes to work while the parent with the beard stays at home. I know it's bullshit, and it's only going to get worse—many North Americans are getting poorer and many of us are getting less like mothers and many of us have conditions, like polycystic ovarian syndrome, that make milk production more challenging. Many of us will never be the best. The best is in part an idea that shores up the gestation and birth and development of a child as a luxury experience, the child as a luxury good. "Failure"—not being the best—is not a function of the inadequacy or ignorance of mothers (or their afterthought analogues); "failure" is a function of the pressures of capitalism.

I LIKE TO STAND IN FRONT OF THE DAIRY CASE at the grocery store for an extra beat, before I buy my milk, to picture the cows who have produced it. I think about the milk production of cows as one line on the x-y axis and the breastfeeding rates of humans as another line on that same axis. We have been rendering one as efficient as possible, to the detriment of that animal, at the same time as we have been rendering one a luxury experience, to the detriment of that animal.

Breastfeeding parents have expressed milk since the 1500s. It got easier in the 1990s when a Swiss company called Medela developed electric pumps—manual pumps are laborious and not very effective, in my experience extracting about two ounces of milk whereas an electric pump extracts something more like three or four. One of the jokes about expressing milk is that—with one's breasts vacuumed into the plastic bullhorns of the pump—it makes one feel like a cow. The pump's suction is stronger and faster for the first two minutes of pumping, and then, once the letdown of milk has been triggered, it relaxes. Like a wind sprint easing into a jog. When a human milks a cow, they first clean and dry her teats. Then they pull gently but firmly until the milk comes. Or they clean and dry her teats and affix a milker—sometimes a vacuum milker, just like the electric pump I used. At farms with robot milkers, the robot cleans and dries the cow, and then the machine uses ultrasound sensors to seek and attach to the cow's teats.

Pumping feels more like being a cow than breastfeeding does, and that says a lot about the relationship between cows and humans, and the way we intercede in the relationship between a cow and her calf—we no longer see the baseline relationship between calving and lactation in cows as one that would lead primarily to a cow feeding her calf directly. In addition, given that the average Canadian consumes about sixty-six litres of milk a year, it also betrays that we take for granted, and are dismissive of, one of our most significant food sources. (It is, of course, always more complicated than that. Wealthy white women used to offload the labour of breastfeeding to wet nurses, often Black women or poorer white women; the legacy of this practice understandably complicates the way a Black woman or a poor white woman with wet nurses in her family tree might think about breastfeeding and pumping—and is another contributing factor to the differing rates of breastfeeding by race.)

Nursing and pumping milk for Sinclair made me reconsider my relationship with dairy. It made me feel more grateful. We started to introduce cow's milk into her diet by mixing it with my milk, topping up each thawed bag of my milk with full-fat cow's milk, straight from the jug in the fridge. After I became a human with a vitamin alarm—salmon oil for mood and joints, B complex to aid with stress—my milk changed colour, shifting from a near-white to a white tinged with goldenrod yellow from the B vitamins. Cows' diets, I learned, also—of course!—affect the colour and composition of their milk. Jersey cows' milk has a higher fat and protein content than that of Holsteins', but they are smaller cows and lower producers, in general, so many large herds of Holsteins will include a couple Jerseys to bump up their milk's fat and protein content. I had accepted that milk came in neat and tidy conventional grocery store packages—skim, 1%, 2%, 3.25%—without ever stopping to question why or how an animal product that comes from hundreds, thousands, millions of animals could be so regularized.

When I pump, I don't feel like a cow, but I do think about cows. Their furry bodies, spotted or warm brown or russet red. Their affability, the way they pick a leader, the way their panoramic eyes follow a field interloper as their heads dip and raise, their jaws working as they chew their cud. I think of the teaching cow at the University of Guelph that we used to pass as we walked from campus over to the mall to get groceries—the infamous cow with a hole in its stomach, the one the aggies plumb to learn about cow feed and cow digestion.

I want to feel a radical kinship with cows, but I haven't earned it. I don't want them to go from one type of Fisher-Price imaginary to another, where they carry narrative or symbolic weight for my feelings about working and pumping and nursing and growth. I have consumed conventional dairy for most of my life, a lifetime that is already a multitude of lifetimes for the cows whose milk has sustained me. Organic milk in a thick glass bottle feels like a bespoke artifact, like a gift of homemade jam versus the Smucker's on sale for $2.99 as a loss leader, but the truth is that the milk we buy now in a four-litre jug for $5.49 is just as much of a gift.

IN OCTOBER, WHEN SINCLAIR IS TEN MONTHS OLD, my milk production dips again. I have a head cold. Ten months is the point at which dairy cows are allowed to go dry for a period, before they are inseminated and calve again. I got my cold from Sinclair—her first. My body, finally shedding the after-effects of gestation, is re-seeking its normal. At work, I bleed through my clothes and feel that my body has betrayed me. I bleed through my clothes at thirty-four years of age and feel irritated, until I realize that bodies change whether or not you gestate a child. And rather than being a cause for concern, my milk production is probably trending downwards because Sinclair is eating more solid food and needs less milk—maybe the anxiety I am feeling is less tied to Sinclair's needs and more a reflection of the fact that I have been fixated on the math of ounces and hours and days and weeks and pounds and grams for so long that it will be hard to let it go, if it is time to let it go. It is October, she is ten months old, and I am so tired that I can't tell if my body is failing me or I am failing my body.

Later, when Sinclair turns one and we celebrate with carrot cake, I should feel relief. My goal was to reach one year of breastfeeding, and I've met my goal. I am tired of pumping but keep developing excuses to push off reducing pumping and feeding sessions. The stash of milk in the freezer comforts me, the equivalent of living mostly paycheque to paycheque but putting aside ten percent of your meagre earnings for rainy-day savings. I am tired of pumping but scared of what it means to be done feeding Sinclair my milk—not because I am afraid of breaking a special bond, because for us nursing is not the best representation of our parent-child relationship—because it signals that she's no longer an infant, that we have passed into a different stage of her life. Of course, she's no longer an infant either way. I could feed her until pre-K and it wouldn't keep her a baby. But imagined kinships and metaphors and magical thinking illuminate internal truths more than they illuminate objective ones.

kai

KAI IS QUEER AND TRANS. They're twenty-four and grew up in Cumberland, on Vancouver Island. They went to school first in Courtenay, and then in Comox. It's small, where they're from, but they liked it. Kai's parents are liberal and well off, and all their friends are liberal, too.

Kai went to two different high schools, and one of them had a GSA, but they never joined. It felt like they couldn't go without outing themselves. They started dating a girl in grade eleven, before they transitioned, but they weren't very open about their relationship. Kai came out to most of their friends in tenth or eleventh grade, but they weren't out to the whole school. When they came out, no one responded negatively, but they didn't exactly feel comfortable about it. They felt nervous.

At first, Kai came out to their parents as gay, and that was a non-issue. Their girlfriend often stayed over. Kai had family friends who were lesbians, and Kai remembers looking up to them.

When Kai was eighteen, they came out to their parents as trans. Kai had talked to their mom about gender when they were younger and trying to figure things out. She was accepting but didn't know how to find resources for them or what to do about it, exactly. She was like, "Well, this is going to be really hard, but I love you, and you should do what you want to do." But Kai's dad wasn't good with it for a long time. Kai's parents had split up by then, and Kai was living with their mom. They had some pretty shitty fights with their dad and stopped talking to him for a while. It was tough, because Kai still lived in the same small town as their dad, and they didn't feel comfortable being around him.

Kai doesn't really know what brought their dad around. Maybe just time. Their dad went to some informational events. They hadn't known anything about what it meant to be trans, but they learned more and came to see that it was a pretty common thing. Kai's dad is really, really loving, so Kai thinks that the fact that Kai didn't want to see him or spend time with him encouraged their dad to figure out how to be accepting. But it did take a while.

Kai's dad is from Germany, and they speak German together. So one thing that can still be tricky is having conversations with him about friends who use they/them pronouns, for example, where Kai doesn't feel like they have the language to talk to him about that. For now, Kai just switches between gender pronouns, because every word is gendered in German, kind of. Even the word "friend" is gendered. Kai doesn't really know how to navigate that with their dad.

Kai's mom's support and understanding have been really affirming. She got them to a therapist, and then to an endocrinologist. Their dad, they remember, came to that appointment too, so he was kind of supportive. But it was really their mom who helped them access resources.

Kai also has a younger sister, but they didn't really grow up together. After their parents split, they both lived with their mom for a little while, but then their sister went away to private school. She wasn't around when Kai started transitioning. Kai remembers her reaction being like, "I'm really stressed with school. Can we not deal with this right now?" She didn't want to talk about it. She became very accepting pretty quickly, but when Kai first came out to her it was a bit difficult. They're good now. They're really close.

Kai moved away from their hometown the year after they transitioned, but they go back there a lot. Now that it's been five years or so, it's less awkward, but they still occasionally run into people, and when that happens they're uncertain if the person will remember who they are, or remember that they transitioned. One time, one of Kai's closest friends, whom they grew up with, had a birthday party. One of Kai's friend's aunts who hadn't seen Kai since they were really young asked if Kai knew their friend from school. And Kai just said, "Uh, yeah," and then walked away. The aunt knew Kai had transitioned, but she just didn't remember them at all. And then when Kai's mom introduced Kai to one of her neighbours a couple years ago, the neighbour said, "I thought you had two daughters." And Kai's mom was like, "Nope."

After Kai finished high school, they took a gap year, then did an outdoor program at a college for a year in Comox. There were maybe seven other people in the program, and they didn't feel comfortable being open about being trans with them, or about being queer. They became friends with a couple people, and they could be a little more open with them, but in general it felt really hard. They didn't feel comfortable around the men in the group.

Kai now lives in Victoria. They spend time with people who are also queer and trans. Their program at school is pretty small, but they feel more comfortable about being openly queer. It's not an environment where they would have to spend a lot of one-on-one time with someone if they weren't okay with Kai being trans. In the outdoors program, the students would be camping together, kayaking for a week. It felt very different.

The other thing that Kai finds a bit easier about being in a bigger city is clothes shopping. They like going to thrift stores, and they really like to dress up and do drag-type stuff. Courtenay is so much smaller, and they feel less comfortable wandering into the women's section there. Or the store they'd go into is owned by someone they know, or there are people in there they know, or their parents know. In Victoria, they have a group of friends they can go shopping with, and there's more anonymity. There are queer events in Victoria, and they can go out and dance and feel free to wear whatever they want.

7

ON CLASS AND WRITING

MY SHIFT AT THE DOWNTOWN MONTREAL LOCATION of the big box bookstore started nightly at ten or eleven p.m. The regular daily employees had left; the customers had left. The escalator whirred, Christmas music was piped in through the store speakers, the store smelled like coffee and nutmeg, scented candles and pine potpourri: empty ambiance, waiting for tomorrow's shoppers. I felt a bit like that mannequin from the eighties TV show *Today's Special*, alive and moving only after everyone else had gone to sleep.

Skids full of stacked boxes filled the tiny storeroom in the store's northwest corner. The job of the night shift workers, broadly speaking, was to empty the skids and move the product onto the floor. We used box cutters and scanners; we sorted books onto one type of rolling cart, and non-books onto another type. We navigated each other's spaces, dodging and bumping and twirling, speaking in a mix of English and French—finding common cultural ground and rolling our eyes at what people were willing to spend their money on. Later, we shelved the candles, scarves, and journals as well as the books: bargain, art, cooking, teen, self-help, business, science, history. Around midnight, when the mall turned the ventilation system off, the store got hot and began to smell like charred grease. Around three a.m., we hit a wall and stopped talking, put our head-phones in. We sat for a minute while reorganizing books at the bottom of a shelf, and had trouble hauling ourselves back up to standing.

I didn't hate my temporary, seasonal, minimum-wage job. And I didn't embed myself like some Canadian version of Mac McClelland, toiling away in service of a tell-all; when I clicked apply a couple months before I started, my intention was to pay my rent. This type of job was nothing new to me. I'd been working since I was fourteen, usually at more than one job at a time. I'd worked as a bike mechanic. I'd worked at Value Village. I'd worked at Subway and Tim Hortons; I'd worked at a vegetarian restaurant and a curry shop and an organic bakery housed in a Jesuit Centre. I'd worked in communications; I'd done print and web design; I'd taught writing at universities. In addition to working overnights, at the time, I was also working as a freelance journalist and a magazine editor.

Earlier in the fall, before I started my overnight shifts, Jonathan Kay, then editor of the Walrus, published a short piece about class and journalism —arguing that social class, not sex or race (as if the three things could be separated cleanly), was the "final frontier" of diversity in Canada. Reception was mixed. (To the magazine's credit, it published a stellar rejoinder to his piece a few days later by Karen K. Ho.) I was one of the people rolling my eyes at his piece: when Kay wrote that, to his knowledge, he'd never worked with a close colleague who'd experienced real hunger, or a serious health condition that went untreated for economic reasons, it struck a frustrated, verge-of-tears chord. *We may not be close, I thought, but I'm right here. I've written for your magazine.*

NEITHER OF MY PARENTS WENT TO UNIVERSITY, no one expected that I would, and my family couldn't offer me any post-secondary financial support. We could have been comfortably lower middle class. We owned two cars, played hockey. There were a number of ways we could have been okay—I see them now, in hindsight, as an adult with agency—but we weren't. My mother was an alcoholic and in control of the finances, and my dad was mostly unaware. When I was a teen, as my mom's alcoholism got worse, I hid the past-due bills for her. I knew our mortgage wasn't getting paid, and we all knew when the hot water got shut off. After we bounced a cheque at the dentist when I was eight, I didn't go back again until I was eighteen.

I started working young and often. Like a lot of people, I knew that a stable life full of what I wanted would require different things from me than it would require from a kid with a tuition fund.

My first priority was to get out of my house. My second priority was to pursue post-secondary education in the liberal arts. In other words, I class-jumped. I got to university, a fish out of water, and gravitated towards other kids like me—ones who came from working- or lower-middle-class backgrounds, talked funny, didn't quite understand the mechanisms of polite academic society. Not all of us adapted, but I did: I learned what constituted appropriate diction; learned what the people who moved in academic circles liked to eat and drink and read and watch; learned what they wore, how they did their hair, what they did and didn't talk about at the seminar or dinner table. I also learned that part of what was required of me after successfully accomplishing my class jump was to not talk about it. Before the term "good cultural fit" came into regular use, I understood intuitively that making the reality of my background invisible to people like Jonathan Kay was just one more compromise I'd need to make if I wanted to succeed.

WRITING NON-FICTION AND JOURNALISM brought about a similar kind of steep and sudden learning curve, and a similar kind of unspoken contract. It isn't news that writing is a hard go, economically speaking. Writers love what we do, and so we do it, but the work is often—especially for the first years of our careers, when we're building our portfolios and really learning our craft—not paid commensurate to our training, skills, or time.

In early 2013, while I was working at Adbusters, I went on a TVOntario panel to talk about consumption: Do North Americans have too much stuff? For the first part of the conversation, I played the role I was supposed to play. (Yes! We do!) But near the end, I started thinking about the working-class friends of mine who'd gone to university yet were still working in food service. I broke my role to acknowledge that I was skeptical about the way we were framing the issue: "The idea of owning a home, to me, and filling it full of stuff, is actually mildly farcical," I said. "It's not something that is part of my reality at all. I live in an apartment. I have a bicycle ... The friends I have who are having kids now, they're living in apartments the same way they did before."

In non-fiction writing, telling the truth—in particular, truths that are open secrets—is valued, yet we're still cautious and cagey when it comes to talking about money. Writers trade on prestige, and talking about how little we're paid lessens that prestige, both institutionally and personally. In addition, showing roughness around the edges—talking in my townie lilt, dressing like I normally would (black jeans, years-old sweatshirt, functional boots), being too honest about who I am or what my home life was like—threatens career consequences in what is already a very difficult and precarious industry. So I get it. I get why we lie, I understand why we obfuscate, I totally and completely support our decision to stand at the canapé table at the magazine or book awards function pretending we know what we're about to delicately coax off a toothpick with our front teeth while sticking to safe conversation topics.

But that's not what life is really like. The big box bookstore, as well as paying me $10.55 an hour, provided a helpful analogy. At night, the divisions between the public and private spaces of the store were porous: we propped all the doors open and ghosted through the doorjambs as if they'd never again require key codes. Similarly, the divisions between my work lives have been porous. I shelved books written by my friends; I moved the magazines I wrote and edited for to the front of the news-stands. I wrote this essay for Hazlitt and, later, unpacked and shelved a box of books from Penguin Random House, Hazlitt's publisher. I loved the work I did for magazines, but it's also true that I worked elsewhere for minimum wage. I know that class is bound up with race and ethnicity and gender and sexuality, that I'm privileged in so many ways, that part of the reason that no one noticed that I class-jumped is because I was mostly able to blend in. I also know that my reality is remarkable only for its commonality—that many of the people reading this will be nodding along.

We need to start speaking openly about class and writing for two reasons: One, so that we can deepen our conversation about diversity, understanding that it's not and will never be enough to add one person or two people or five people to our mastheads or panel discussions—rather, we have to change the structure of our organizations and our conversations so that they suit a much broader range of people. (English can borrow 1 million words from other languages and still be English; to become French or German, its grammar must change, too.)

Two, so that we can come to terms with the impact of how we value writing, financially speaking. A lot of very talented writers and editors in Canada—some of whom we'd consider at the top of their game in terms of craft—make ends meet by working low-paid, part-time jobs. Still more people who would be talented writers and editors never get the chance to work as writers and editors at all—because they couldn't afford tuition or student debt, couldn't afford to do unpaid internships, couldn't afford low-paid entry-level jobs in high-priced cities.

This is the reality we live in. If we're not okay with it—if we want to pay more than lip service to diversity in media—then we will need to increase municipal and provincial and federal funding for arts and journalism. We will need to offer paid internships, and living wages. We'll need to remove the social penalties for talking about money, and all of us—even those whose parents are still covering their rent—will need to talk about money.

ben

BEN IS QUEER AND A SCORPIO. He was born in 1980 and raised in Prince George, in northern BC. Prince George is in a bowl, so there's a nice, convenient, disgusting temperature inversion that means that all of the town's pulp mill fumes get trapped. Ben remembers standing on the university campus, right outside of the bowl, and looking over the town and seeing where the blue sky met the grey sky. It's an industry town: pulp mill, logging. It's been hit hard, economically. More since Ben left.

Ben went back to Prince George a week and a half ago, for the first time in fourteen years. The weird Catholic store is still there, Ave Maria. Ben drove by the library where he used to work. The sex shop has been there for thirty years. Ben had to have a work lunch, which ended up being in a restaurant right across the street from where he ran when he was getting gay-bashed one night. His co-workers were like, "Downtown's so great," and Ben was like, "Sure."

When he was growing up in Prince George, the town felt grim and boring and small. There were queer people, and he was friends with other queer people, but it wasn't necessarily safe to be super open. In Ben's experience, it was really weird to be around other queer people. He'd be out and about with friends, and they wouldn't know exactly when it was acceptable or not to be visibly queer. Sometimes they'd forget to be vigilant and lose the cues.

There were 1,500 kids in Ben's high school. He was in drama club and the International Baccalaureate program. Two of his best friends were queer, but they didn't talk about it at first. Ben told his friend Eric in grade eleven, and then he told his friend Andrew later on. Ben's high school crush, who he thought was straight, was not straight, so they ended up dating a couple years later.

There was a GALA, a Gay and Lesbian Association. They held a monthly dance party and Ben went to a couple of them. But he had a really bad experience because there were creepy old guys who tried to pick him up, so he didn't go back for a long time. And then there was a lesbian-run pie company. That was the extent of the town's queerness.

Ben lived with his parents in a suburban area, in a decent-sized house. His mom was an elementary school teacher and his dad did car inspections for BC Rail. They were both involved in the local theatre community. Ben's dad directed and acted, and his mom did production and makeup and acting. Ben came out to them at nineteen, which was probably six years after he figured it out. He didn't require much from them emotionally. His dad had found him looking at porn when he was about sixteen, so he must have known something.

Ben applied to the University of Victoria to study creative writing, but he didn't get in the first time. He decided that a geography degree at the University of Northern British Columbia was more practical. Looking back, he was maybe a little scared about leaving. He wasn't totally ready.

Ben's time at UNBC was interesting. There was a cluster of people who were all really close friends. Most of them had known each other in high school. They were all straight and slept with each other an embarrassing amount. It was a lot of drama. Ben went to raves. For the first year and a half, Ben was a sober raver. But then: he came out to his parents on a Thursday and went out to the Ironhorse Pub, which was a shitty redneck bar, but they were rebranding as a pub by day, club by night. All the ravers went there on Thursdays, and there was a DJ. He did E that night for the first time. Coming out to his parents had felt like a huge, massive release. After telling them, he didn't really know what direction everything was going to go in.

Ben's mom is an alcoholic. He grew up not being able to predict her emotional responses to things, and that informs a lot of his anxiety generally. Coming out was a big haze. He wasn't sure how his parents were going to react, how they were going to take it. Queer issues never came up in conversation, so he never knew where they stood. Ben's dad has always been a very stoic, emotionally closed-off person. Their reactions were very different. His mom was very surprised. Ben had never had a girlfriend, but he had a close female friend, Krista, he was always hanging out with, and his mom was always trying to see if we were together. His mom was worried about promiscuity and STDs, and AIDS was implied even though she didn't say it outright. Ben's dad just asked if he had a boyfriend.

Ben didn't have a boyfriend at the time, but about a week after he told his parents, he lost his virginity. It was a crazy month. Ben had started talking to a guy who had a boyfriend. The guy broke up with his boyfriend the next week, and then they hooked up. But the guy only wanted casual stuff, so Ben hooked up with someone else. And then he hooked up with the boyfriend.

Then he started dating his high school crush, who was going to school in Vancouver, and that made it easier for Ben to move away. Ben got into UVic the second time he applied, and he moved to Victoria with his friend Krista.

Even after Ben arrived in Victoria, all of the small-town programming was still there, and it took him a long time to feel like he could be himself. After he moved he picked up this guy named Cameron at the lesbian bar. Cameron was visiting for the weekend from Vancouver. They met up for a date and went down to the Inner Harbour, and because there were people around, Ben wasn't comfortable being affectionate or holding Cameron's hand, and he was keeping his distance. It took about five years for Ben to feel comfortable being visibly affectionate with someone in public, without holding back.

That discomfort has never really gone away completely. Even now, Ben and his partner, Michael, are always very aware of the situations they're in. This past fall, they went to Williams Lake to visit Ben's dad and stepmother for Thanksgiving, and suddenly they had to think about, "We're renting a hotel room with one bed. Is that going to be cool to deal with?" and "Let's maintain a healthy physical distance at all times." He'd forgotten how much psychological pressure there is all the time in those small-town spaces. It's more situational in Vancouver. Basically, if there are loud, drunk straight guys around, he'll immediately put up that wall.

Disclosing and coming out is always a thing that you have to do, over and over again. Ben ended up coming out in the middle of a job interview once, to give context to his response to a question about work with marginalized communities. You'd think that it would get easier to come out, but it kind of doesn't. You're always waiting for half a second, to see what the reaction is going to be. Even if there's no indication that it will be bad. Occasionally, people still assume Ben's straight. He feels like he's very obviously queer, and as he's gotten older, he really enjoys leaning into being queer, but it comes up. For a while, the CEO at his current job thought that Ben and one of his female colleagues were secretly dating. He's been working pretty closely with the CEO for about three years now, but only in the last six months has he started talking about his husband, being very clear about being queer.

Ben hadn't thought about what being an old queer could be or look like until probably the past two years, when he finally saw old gay male characters on TV shows. The two that stand out are Martin Sheen and Sam Waterston's characters on *Grace and Frankie*. Ben knows queer elders, but he hadn't totally internalized it. For Ben's generation, in some ways it feels like they're just getting older queer elders now. So many men in the generation before Ben's generation died.

Ben prefers to identify as queer rather than gay for several reasons. He likes the word—aesthetically, he finds it more pleasing. And it implies a greater economic group. He also feels like everyone across the rainbow is part of his community. The word has a lot of vastness to it. It's been academically accepted for more than a decade. When he hears younger people now saying that queer is a slur, it feels loaded and TERF-y.

Ben always thinks about that scene in *Chasing Amy* where Amy's friends get mad at her for dating a man. She's no longer in the social position that they thought she was. It's complicated. Queer identity is inherently destabilizing, he thinks, even if sometimes what's being destabilized *is* queer identity.

8

THE BOTTOMLESS PIT OF
SELF-LOATHING / A PEAK

THERE'S A MOMENT IN THE ROCK CLIMBING MOVIE *Free Solo* where Alex Honnold and his girlfriend, Sanni McCandless, hit a rough spot in their relationship. McCandless doesn't understand why Honnold feels the need to risk his life by free soloing El Capitan—that is, scaling a 3,000-foot-high granite monolith in Yosemite National Park without any ropes or safety gear. She can't quite comprehend why it's so important to him. To the filmmakers, later, Honnold explains that he and McCandless are very different people. "For Sanni," he says, "the point of life is happiness. To be with people that make you feel fulfilled and to have a good time." For Honnold, the point of life is performance. "Nothing good happens in the world," he says, "by being happy and cozy."

In another part of *Free Solo*, it becomes clear that Honnold grew up with parents who weren't very affectionate. His mother hasn't been impressed by anything he's achieved. "My mom's favourite sayings are '*presque ne compte pas*,' almost doesn't count, or 'good enough isn't,'" he says, followed a moment later by a sentence fragment: "The bottomless pit of self-loathing." It seems like he's internalized the need to seek perfection, the moment when he's won, when there is nothing better. He's dedicated years of his life to reaching this moment; there is a film crew, composed of his friends, committed to putting it to tape. Alex thinks that if he dies while he's climbing, everyone will be sad for a time, and then they'll get over it. But onscreen, in the movie, his friends struggle with the idea of him falling. They grapple with the idea that they could be training a camera on him, then witness their friend plunging through the frame, and that the pressure of people watching will encourage him to try before he's ready. They read his actions for the underlying meaning; when, in the fall of 2016, Honnold halts his first free solo attempt of El Cap—"Um, I think I'm bailing," he says, over the radio—*Free Solo* co-director Jimmy Chin is buoyed by the fact that Honnold feels he can abandon an attempt when he's not ready for it, even with people watching, even with cameras on him.

I WATCH CLIMBING MOVIES for the same reason I read about religions: I want to understand how people believe what they believe, and why they do what they do. I try to understand, in part, because I will never understand—understanding can't really come from study, unless study provokes an epiphany. But I keep watching anyway.

Honnold regularly completes routes without ropes, harness, or protective gear. He's climbed a lot of routes this way: Astroman and the Rostrum in Yosemite; Moonlight Buttress in Zion National Park in Utah; El Sendero Luminoso in El Potrero Chico, Mexico. *Free Solo* documents the months and years leading up to his final, successful attempt on El

Capitan. The cliff looms over a calm, bird-filled meadow bisected by the Merced River in Yosemite. Will, Sinclair, and I went to Yosemite last Christmas and stayed in a lodge with Will's family. We stood in that same meadow, marvelling at El Cap, which draws you upwards the same way a small part of your body, when you're standing on a bridge, or over a crevasse or waterfall, draws you down. Fear, revulsion, pull.

I USED TO THINK THAT I WOULD, for some short period of time, like to be the best at something. Even as I thought that there usually wasn't someone who was the best at something, but rather there was probably a field of very good people. It's possible I co-won a math contest at my high school once, and it's also possible that I only ever came in second—I have a memory of standing on crutches in front of my high school's sign, out by the main road, with one or two other kids. Of appearing in our local paper for doing well on the annual math contest, just after I'd gotten knee surgery. I didn't save the clipping, and no one else in my family did, either. I gave all my school certificates and medals to a grandparent who is now very old and no longer speaks to me because I don't speak to my mother. I gave them away because my grandparents were able to feel an uncomplicated pride at the time, and I wanted to feel it vicariously through them.

The same part of me who would like to be the best, who also says I never will be, can rationalize why this doesn't matter: even if I was the best in my school, I wasn't the best in the district, or the region. And I should not be thinking about high school, about a subject I didn't pursue past high school, in order to find an estimation of myself that is good enough to live with. What I have in common with Alex Honnold is not any sort of specified skill set, or even dedication. It's the bottomless pit of self-loathing. Can I blame my own parents for infecting me with a drive towards achievement? My father is nothing but a sunbeam of praise (I don't trust it, but that's not his fault), and his core values, as a semi-reformed anarchic hippie who cares more for cheese and music festivals and good beer than for almost anything else, are almost diametrically opposed to achievement. Although my mother didn't seem to care either way about much else, she did always want me to lose weight and be pretty. And I do remember experiencing, in elementary school, the satisfaction of receiving a high grade—it felt like some small corner of worth that no one could take away from me. But the feeling receded almost as soon as I felt it, because I could always do better. Bottomless pit!

WHEN WILL AND I MOVED TO NEW YORK—I was going to stay for as long as a Canadian can stay on vacation, Will for nine months—I found an old single-speed Dutch city cruiser bike on Craigslist. It was reasonably priced because it needed a new wheel and brake pads. I took the train out to Long Island, gave a middle-aged man a fistful of cash, and brought the bike back to Brooklyn, where we were staying that month. I had the wheel replaced, swapped out the brake pads, and tried to ride the bike. It was heavy and required a fully upright riding position. I thought its built-for-slowness would encourage me to coast peacefully around Brooklyn, taking things in rather than focusing on reaching a destination. In Vancouver, on my road bikes, moderately hunched over the handlebars, I rode until my breath came in little puffs and my thighs burned and sweat collected on my forehead. The cruiser was supposed to turn me into a different, more chill person.

Except that I couldn't stand being so upright and going so slow—I hated the bike almost immediately. I sold it to a tall young woman who was in New York from Amsterdam. I watched her test ride it, sliding on and off the bike easily, like they were old friends, and then I took her money, maybe less than I'd originally given the man on Long Island, and watched her ride off. Later that week, I bought a rigid-frame nineties mountain bike at a shop on the Lower East Side. The guy who owned the shop had volunteered at a co-op where I'd worked as a mechanic. He gave me a break on the price after I walked him through the fixes I would need to do to bring the bike back as close as it could get to its initial state of nineties perfection. It was the type of bike another mechanic would like but the general population of the city would not. I could ride it hard, until my breath came in little puffs and my thighs burned and sweat collected on my forehead.

IF THE IDEA IS THAT YOU DIE EITHER WAY, and the question that follows concerns how you would like to live your life—contentedly or in search of one moment of perfection, slowly and happily or mostly miserable but sometimes the best—I can't imagine consciously choosing to be miserable most of the time. I especially can't imagine being someone who doesn't believe in life after death and living a life that is more oriented towards posterity than the days and weeks and months I'm lucky enough to be here. I can't imagine it, even though I am often living it without thinking. If I wasn't afraid of death, or of the pain that would have come in old age if I'd kept pushing my body, would my value system shift? If I felt like I could be the best at any one thing, even for a short period of time, would

I try for it even if I knew it wouldn't bring me what I really wanted—stable self-worth, an enduring feeling of contentedness?

AFTER I LEFT NEW YORK FOR MONTREAL, I walked fifty minutes from Côte-des-Neiges, around Mount Royal, to work overnights downtown. As the fall and winter progressed, it got colder, and the cold tickled the outer edges of my thighs, which had gotten slightly frostbitten once before, in Guelph, Ontario, also from walking to work. The feeling was like pinpricks, like the pain of sensation returning after windburn. I did it because I didn't have money for the bus, and because the cold and the exercise set the perspective for my workday, reminding me that life existed more dramatically outside of the oppressive warmth and Christmas carols and paper cuts of the bookstore. And because I could, because I should. Because if I took the bus instead of walking, when I could reasonably walk, who would I be?

Later, when I was earning enough, and living cheaply enough, I could make the choice to sometimes take transit. And then I got pregnant. Instead of pushing myself physically, I redirected my energies into pushing myself to work as much as I could. My urge to work, which had always been strong, driven by anxiety, got worse in pregnancy. I received a grant and was accepted to a month-long residency, but I still found myself unable to say no to freelance contracts—I couldn't yet picture what life with a baby would even be like. Freelance cheques often took a long time to come, and financially it felt a little like running to the next bus stop after missing the bus, only to miss it once more. The only calculation that made sense was to work so that I was making, on paper, more than I'd need to live—so that if an outlet took six months, or two years, to pay me, I could still cover my rent. Another version of the bottomless pit: even after I was able to save some money, I ran the numbers in my head over and over, calculating how many bad months it would take until I'd be out on the street. What if things became too complicated for me to make enough money through working? What would we do then?

At the beginning of the pregnancy, when I was biking alone, I still felt like a wound-up top set loose every time I got into the saddle, frustrated by the way the lights and traffic of the city forced me to slow down. Eventually, though, my belly grew. My belly grew and I could feel the fetus kicking, and I switched bikes from my favourite, fastest bike to my more relaxed touring bike. My sit bones widened; I bought a new saddle. By the time I was visibly pregnant, I didn't mind going slow. In fact, going slow felt, for the first time, like the exact right thing to do. I called the rides enceint(e) et lent(e). Will and I would set a destination and go there at a crawl, getting passed by middle-aged men in spandex on carbon frames, by couriers, by newlyweds on hybrids, by hipsters on ill-advised fixies. As I pedalled, more slowly than I ever had before, I thought being pregnant had permanently changed me, re-established my existence to be in a place where I could enjoy slowness.

And it had changed me, but only temporarily. Only because my body was housing another body, and the care I wanted to give to that other body briefly superseded my most basic compulsions, quieting, for a while, even the bottomless pit. While I was pregnant, I enjoyed going slow and noticing more of the world around me. But after Sinclair arrived and my body healed and she was strong, I became, again, the type of person who likes to go fast but wants to go slow. The days again felt like they were peeling off, faster and faster, one by one by one.

BEFORE MY CHILDHOOD BROKE ME, I was the type of kid for whom fifteen minutes could feel like twenty-four hours. I daydreamed constantly, and I'd mapped an entire imaginary world onto my elementary school playground, complete with imaginary friends because I didn't have many in real life. After Sinclair was born and my neuroses returned—looking to become a better parent—I wondered who I would be if I hadn't had to extinguish that part of myself, and what I could do to bring part of it back.

Ironically, the same park where Alex Honnold achieved the pinnacle of his climbing career provided me with a potential way forward: I'd brought no laptop with me to Yosemite for Christmas with Will's family, and cell reception was weak and patchy. I'd scheduled no work. We had nothing to do but wander and hike and ensure that Sinclair, newly turned one, stayed fed.

My brain calmed down. My entire nervous system calmed down. (I think people call this a vacation.)

Back in Powell River, a few months later, we started the first seeds inside for our new vegetable garden. The seeds required water, sunlight, warmth, and time. They grew slowly, then in spurts. We dug out garden beds and planted the seedlings outside. The peppers inched along; the tomatoes shot up like weeds. At a thrift shop, we bought Sinclair, who was now walking, a small yellow watering can so that she could contribute. The garden, like Sinclair, became an external living thing I could care for and watch grow. It was resistant to impatience. I could putter around in it, weeding and watering and snapping off aging leaves, soaking up the sun and going back into the house smelling like dirt and fresh air. It became Sinclair's favourite place to hang out.

I think, as I get older, I've started to loathe myself less. The life I've made with Will, for Sinclair, is more secure than the life that I had when I was younger. I don't need to strive as much, or worry as much. I can slow down by going outside; I can learn to care for myself by caring for Sinclair, by caring for my plants, by resisting the pull of a peak when I know that all it will do is underscore how far into the pit I could fall.

adam

ADAM IS THIRTY, GAY, AND QUEER. He grew up in the Head of Chezzetcook, a town on the eastern shore of Nova Scotia. It's a small Acadian community. Adam is Acadian but doesn't speak French. He wishes, now, that he'd studied it at school.

The area where he grew up was gloomy, very foggy all the time. Adam always jokes that he didn't see the sun for the first twenty years of his life. The gloominess informed his attitude of general malaise.

Adam went to a high school that served nearly the entire eastern shore. Some people bussed for an hour and a half to get to school. There weren't a lot of opportunities for him to see his friends outside of school. There was no public transit. There were no sidewalks. There was one highway with streets off of it. It wasn't a place where you could walk to your friend's house or see people if you didn't have a car.

Adam grew up in a two-bedroom bungalow off the highway. He was really into movies when he was a kid. He always brought the free magazines from the movies home and would cut out the full-page movie posters. His bedroom walls were covered in posters for terrible movies he hadn't even seen. He also had the *Kill Bill* poster. He downloaded *Kill Bill* and watched it really tiny because he wasn't supposed to be watching it. *Kill Bill* is what made him realize movies could be art, which seems silly to him now, but it was important at the time.

Because he wasn't out when he was growing up, it wasn't a terribly difficult time, but that was only because he wasn't really being himself. He was just doing his homework, having his girlfriend over, doing what he thought he was supposed to do. Adam was a big people-pleaser, and he was anxious about what people would think of him.

There was a Gay–Straight Alliance at his school, but it appeared to be all allied people. Some of the people in the alliance did eventually come out, but at the time, there were no out people in his community at all. Adam had one friend in the GSA. They're both out now, but she wasn't then. In Adam's memory, it was his friend who really championed and pushed the GSA.

Adam came out when he was nineteen and was basically already leaving Head of Chezzetcook. He lived at home for two years of university, because he was trying not to take out too many loans. But he started to feel like he was getting to a point where he was coming to terms with who he was, and he needed to figure out how to deal with that. He started to tell his friends. He was also tired of staying on people's couches and wanted his own place.

Adam moved to Halifax with three friends, into a place on the corner of a main intersection in the city. It was not the nicest apartment, but it was his apartment, and he could do what he wanted. All he had at first was an air mattress and a record player—and one Antony and the Johnsons record. So he would just sit on his little air mattress, in his little basement room, with one small window, listening to "One Dove."

Adam doesn't go back home very often, because it feels a bit weird. When he came out to his parents at twenty-three or so it didn't go well. His relationship with them is still basically where it was when that happened. They had two conversations about it, and then just stopped talking about it. On holidays, he goes home, and it's weird because they pretend nothing's happening. Siblings and cousins will have their partners there, and there'll be gifts for partners. And it's just, like, Adam sitting in the corner, feeling like a crazy person, because he has this entire, very rich life, but he can't share that with his family, because it's too painful to talk about. So he talks about trucks, or a new drill he got at work that's really useful. It's easier than saying, "I'm actually really devastated by the current state of our relationship."

Adam has a partner in Halifax. It surprises him how little things changed with his family after he came out. They're all still posturing. It's hard because people are always asking him, "What are you doing? What's going on?" And anything that's interesting in Adam's life is usually queer in some way, so he says, "Nothing." But he's actually making his first short film. He's been doing stand-up comedy for two years. He's written three plays. But it's all gay, so he can't really share it.

The people in his family who are Adam's age are more supportive and comfortable to be around. His brother's a good guy who's really defended Adam to his family. And he always asks after Adam's partner. Adam doesn't see his cousins as much. Last January, Trixie Mattel, one of the winners of

RuPaul's *Drag Race*, came to Halifax to do a comedy show. Pride brought her in and asked Adam and a couple of other people to open for her. It was such a cool thing., and Adam was really excited about it. He didn't realize until afterwards, but a couple of his cousins were at the show. He got a message from his cousin that was like, "I thought it was really cool!"

Adam thinks his is a crux generation because they grew up during a time of a lot of technological change. The older generations interacted with each other differently, whereas with Adam's generation, a lot of relationships started online, but it was a lot of clunky beta-testing of garbage technology. And then this new generation of younger queer people have all this incredible advanced technology, and everything is available to them.

Adam thinks that the millennial queer generation was, in some ways, lucky to have a really singular experience. Even though it's tricky. Because they get to talk about it and create art about it that says: "Our lives are really weird and here's why."

The other thing he thinks is weird is the way millennials were encouraged to go to university to gain future employment. Community college and trades weren't presented to Adam as options because he was good at school. Adam looks around and it feels like his entire generation is just, like, wildly educated and talented and living in basements.

Until a few years ago, Adam was very involved in queer advocacy work in Nova Scotia, working with the Rainbow Action Project, and he's talked with a lot of queer people. He really likes talking with elder queer people, just to hear what their experiences have been. He always tries to keep in mind that we lost a generation, because the AIDS crisis decimated the community and disconnected the generations of queer people.

9

WHAT I LEARNED TRUEING BIKE WHEELS

BEFORE THE HEAD OF A BOLT ROUNDS, you can feel it beginning to give. If you teach your hands—or learn to listen to them—you'll notice a moment, or a series of moments, as the Allen key presses into and turns the bolt, before the rounding happens. What should be firm begins not to be. There is a slippage between making better and making worse.

When I first started fixing bikes, I rounded a lot of bolts. Before I learned to look to see if there was rust, or if the edges of the bolt head's hole were already a little worn—before I learned that other mechanics were not just picking any five-millimetre Allen key off the wall; they were picking the five-millimetre Allen key with the crispest edges—I rounded a lot of bolts. I did not feel them begin to give; I felt them go.

If a bolt rounds, there are a few ways to extract it, but my favourite way, whenever possible, is to take a small handsaw and score the bolt head until it has a new point of tool contact, one that will work for a flathead screwdriver. It feels like failure to round a bolt head, but if you are given the choice between the bolt head rounding and the bolt snapping off in its place—if the person riding the bike has generally left it outside over a wet Vancouver winter and is now trying to make it rideable again, if the chain oil you dripped hopefully down along the bolt threads has not worked well enough—you want the bolt head to round.

What you are trying to cultivate is knowledge of what the bolt wants, what the bike wants, how the tool feels. The tool is an extension of your hand, your arm, your body. To know the tool, you need to know your body. If you are used to turning your body mostly off, and then living in a small corner of it, you will need to learn to live in the whole of it again. At least for the period of time it will take to not round the bolt.

I WAS THIN FOR THE FIRST TIME IN MY LIFE prior to working as a bike mechanic. The way I got thin was to get sick. I ate two bites and felt overfull. I ate and it hurt—my stomach, my intestines, my torso, something, it hurt. I had gained weight on lithium a couple years earlier, and some but not all of the weight disappeared. When I started losing weight, it was easier to buy clothing for my communications job. I felt sick and people complimented me and asked me for my weight-loss secrets. The secret was that I had no appetite and no longer received hunger cues. I went, instead, straight from mild, unending nausea to dizziness.

I went to a doctor, who noticed my glands were swollen. She sent me for blood tests, but everything came back mostly normal. She sent me for more tests, and when those came back mostly normal, she suggested I go to a naturopath. By then my work was suffering because the not-eating had begun to affect my cognitive functioning. The weight kept coming off. The compliments kept coming, too.

At the time, I had a terrible relationship with my mother, but we were still speaking. I was due to visit her. I was the smallest I'd ever been in my adult life, the smallest I'd been since the seventh grade. I was running, but that was secondary to the not-eating. I was running, but when I ran, before the pace of the run took over, a heaviness had begun to press on my chest. That heaviness was iron deficiency. But the size on my pants was the smallest it had ever been, and for once, it felt like the stores were making the clothing for me, or someone me-analogous. My mother and I had been diet collaborators—that is, together we defined my diets, and she helped me learn how to hate my body and want another one—since I was eight. None of the diets ever worked because my appetite always overrode my desire to melt away and reveal my true thin self, but the universe had finally smiled down on me with a mystery digestive issue.

I was due to go to my mother's house, and I thought, *I won. I'm thin and you finally have nothing on me. Fuck you.*

My boyfriend at the time was moderately uncomfortable with our positionalities in the relationship. I had never learned how or wanted to be someone's girlfriend. I wasn't even a girl. Once, when we disagreed, he got as frustrated as a toddler and said that of course I was right—I was smarter than him and he was just stupid and he'd never be right. This was a sentiment I'd heard from my mother, too, but hers usually came as part of a tornado of offence. My boyfriend's, it took me a long time to realize, was more like a killdeer's. He would lie on the ground and pretend to be hurt, but it was really a trick. We were together when I got sick and began to shrink. My shrinking body was convenient in the context of our relationship. I encouraged other parts of myself to shrink, too.

As I got thin, my grandma Garcia, who'd lived through a world war and then postwar rationing, said I looked more like myself with some weight on me. "It's too much," she said about my thinness, and I thought she was probably constitutionally oriented to desire some bodily buffer in case hard times returned. And my best friend told me that her mother was confused. Her mother said, "I thought it was part of andrea, to be big and strong."

At the time, I was living in a corner of my body where these things were not really reaching me. But in addition to running, I started strength training. Before going to bed with my boyfriend, I did push-ups and sit-ups on his floor. My vertebrae made unpleasant contact with the hardwood.

"Tell your mom I still want to be strong," I told my best friend.

I FIRST BECAME A BIKE MECHANIC after volunteering at a co-op for a couple years, and after I slowly, and with a lot of help, built my own bike. There is a tome called the Big Blue Book of Bicycle Repair, published by a major bike tool manufacturer and written by a mechanic called C. Calvin Jones; when I was hired as a junior mechanic, I read it from cover to cover. If I didn't understand something, I diagrammed it on paper until I did. Jones is a careful, thorough writer, encouraging would-be mechanics to cultivate knowledge about their bodies as well as bicycles. Early in the book, he outlines how to set up a bike repair area: make your bench deep enough to hold a wheel; bolt the bench to the floor and to a wall; "move the work area of the bike closer to you, rather than bending over. Save your back for riding."

The things I understood theoretically did not, at first, translate into real-world experience. There are a million different kinds of bike shops, and they all have their quirks; the quirk of a co-op is that a very wide range of bikes in many stages of disrepair roll or are carried into the shop. It's a learning space, and learners are harder on tools, which degrade more quickly as a result. What I learned from the textbook all of a sudden had many more variables. I felt like I'd landed in the deep end of the pool, was told to do a butterfly stroke, and could only muster a mix of floating and front crawl. I wanted to keep up with my fellow mechanics and was very conscious of how many fixes I was doing per day, in comparison to them, which should not have been my focus. Three months in, the senior mechanic who'd been assigned to mentor me took me out onto the grass for a meeting: if I didn't shift the way I was approaching my fixes, I wouldn't make it out of my probationary period.

So I shifted. I took things more slowly. I asked for help when I wasn't sure what I was doing. I double-checked my work. I let my body learn what my brain knew already; I let myself pay close attention to the variables that affect any given fix. After a few weeks, it felt like something fundamental had changed.

Throughout this period of learning, I was slowly gaining weight—I had been diagnosed with a stomach condition, cut a few types of food from my diet, and finally began to heal. Before that, in my period of thinness, I'd stopped menstruating. I'd broken up with the guy who liked me smaller. I'd broken up with him, and then, when I visited the place where we'd met, he sexually assaulted me in my sleep. I learned how to fix bikes as I processed this betrayal, during a time when I flinched whenever someone touched my arm, or my shoulder, or brushed against me on the bus. During a time when gaining weight meant reconciling with my body. I gained weight past the point where I needed it to begin menstruating again, past the point where I would then have drawn a line between too thin and ideal. I let my body find the place where it was comfortable; I prioritized that comfort. Learning how best to position my body to use the tools to fix the bikes was a reciprocal process: I embodied larger and larger corners of my body until I was able to live in it fully, as if it were my own, as if my embodied experience was what mattered the most to me.

MY FAVOURITE THING TO DO as a bike mechanic is true wheels. When I began volunteering, my task was often to tackle the wheel pile—a heap of donated wheels that would accumulate in a cold, concrete corner of the shop. (Most of the shop's corners were cold and concrete; if it rained too much, moisture made it through the cracks in the ceiling.) To tackle the wheel pile, I first removed all the wheels that were not fixable, or worth fixing—wheels with steel rims, broken spokes, and cracked axles; wheels with worn-down braking surfaces. Sometimes the tire was salvageable, or the hub, or the axle. Next I had to identify wheels that were fixable—hubs that could be overhauled, and wheels that could be trued.

At first, much of this distinction was noise, with no discernible signal. And then it became clearer, and I couldn't remember what it was like to not know—steel rims were shiny and smooth, heavier than alloy; a certain type of sticking, when revolving the wheel around its axle, probably meant the axle was too bent or broken to bother with, unless it was a really rare type of wheel.

Even as I got better at trueing wheels—placing them on the trueing stand, adjusting the spoke tension until the wheel approached something closer to as good as it would get—there was sometimes a period where what I was learning from the wheel felt mostly like noise. I'd make an adjustment only to find that something unexpected had happened elsewhere as a result. Later, when I taught mechanics and had to verbalize everything useful I'd learned, this made perfect sense. While I was learning, it felt instead like a fog that settled and lifted only when I'd figured out how to move beyond making things confusingly worse before they got better.

To true wheels, I sat on a tall stool by the stand, or stood above it. As a paid mechanic I took as many work chits as possible that involved wheel trues or hub overhauls, but if I'm honest, it's even more enjoyable when I'm volunteering, or fixing my own wheels, and can go as slow as I want. Making tiny adjustments to the spoke nipples, detensioning the wheel, placing it back on the stand and starting over. When part of the way I paid my rent was to work as a mechanic, fixing wheels offered a type of quiet and focus I might not get at any other point of the day in a busy shop. It offered a way to return things to almost perfect that was visible, and relatively fast—but it also taught me a lesson of discernment in when to stop before going too far.

The micro-movements of wheel trueing fell into a skill set that was already comfortable for me, using the fine motor skills I'd honed working in kitchens and making zines. Wheel trueing was a bit of a cheat. What was harder were the mid-range movements, figuring out how and when to apply force, and how much force to apply.

The same mechanic who'd taught me how to sort through the wheel pile—and how to tell a V-brake from a cantilever brake, how to find the best and right derailleur for any given bike—also taught me about leverage.

How to position my body to get the most force from the least effort. This was a skill that came in handy often at the shop where we worked, a community co-op where many of the bikes we fixed were owned by students who had no place to keep them but outdoors. On one side of the shop wall we kept several lengths of steel pipe, which we slid over a tool to extend its length to get more leverage when the part the tool was attached to had become seized onto the bike. A mechanic from an earlier era had developed a tool for when the fixed cup of a bottom bracket did not want to budge from the frame. There were large Y-shaped pieces of steel I knew only by their nicknames—"tuning forks" and "pickle forks"—that we occasionally employed to forcefully extract cranks. These were to be used with the understanding that they were really a last resort, because there was always a chance that while trying to remove the cranks you could accidentally damage the frame.

I'd learned a bit about fixing bikes from the Big Blue Book. But then, in practice, I had to learn everything all over again with my body, by trying and failing, in a long and challenging and rewarding and sometimes sore and painful process. Cold, wet steel frames, finger pinches, dropped tools, seized parts, fixable parts, unfixable ones. Less technical stuff, I learned later: Most of my workmates ate once, in the middle of the day, large meals they brought from home or bought on campus. I fared better if I followed my own body's rhythms, eating a mid-morning snack. I was good at teaching classes, and I liked my job better if I had a slightly varied schedule. By the time I left—I left my job because it was time to leave Vancouver—I was a half-decent mechanic, and the most important parts of the knowledge lived in my large-again body.

When I left, I volunteered at a workshop for women and trans people—women including trans and cis women, trans people including non-binary folks and trans men who preferred to learn with women and other trans people—in New York, then worked at a shop in Montreal before finally volunteering at another co-op, where I passed on what I'd learned from everyone I'd learned from. When I got pregnant, my growing belly changed my relationship again with the way I positioned myself at the trueing stand and with the tools. It wasn't as much of a process, that time, to understand how to change. I followed my body's cues, adapted as I needed to without having to think much about it, just by inhabiting my large and growing and only body.

soraya

SORAYA IS THIRTY-NINE. She and her brother were both born in England. Both of her parents are British doctors. Canada had a doctor shortage, and her parents didn't want to raise them in London, so they moved to Kanata, Ontario, when Soraya was two. A couple years later, they moved to Ottawa. Then, when she was eleven or twelve, they moved back to England for a year before returning to Canada, to Alberta.

All of Soraya's formative teen years—twelve to eighteen—took place in Calgary. She left for university in Montreal for a year, and then ended up in Toronto.

In Calgary, her gym teacher was the face of Alberta beef. She remembers seeing billboards with him in the cowboy hat, the flannel shirt. Moustache. Sam Elliott in the remake of A Star Is Born. That kind of look. All the guys Soraya went to school with had that look. Good-looking enough, masculine enough, but it didn't really do anything for her.

Soraya wasn't attracted to those guys, but she was attracted to guys, that was clear, so it felt like maybe she didn't need to question things any further. But then she had an experience in high school. She must have been sixteen. She was in her friend's basement, watching TV or a movie, and they were doing something with their hands. And Soraya got this feeling of being attracted to her. It wasn't reciprocated. Her friend is very straight. But in her head Soraya was like, *This is because we're friends. That happens.* And then she became friends with a girl at twenty-one or so, and that was the point when she was like, *I feel like I'm attracted to this person.* She wanted to be friends, but she was also attracted to her. Her friend had a bit of fluidity herself, but she also had a boyfriend. It wasn't just like, "No!" It was a whole conversation.

Soraya doesn't feel like she had the language back then that exists now. She felt like she was straight but attracted to this one particular girl. When people say, "I just love who I love," and "I don't have labels," Soraya feels like that's where that comes from. She remembers talking to her brother, who teaches philosophy, and her mom, because her friendship with that person when she was twenty-one broke up. It was incendiary, and Soraya thinks it was probably her fault. Her mom said, "Well, you were always in love with her, anyway." And Soraya was like, "What? I was not." But then she was like, "Oh, well, yeah, maybe I was." Soraya had written a piece about that friendship-breakup, and everyone was like, "You're gay for your friend, you're gay for your friend" and she was like, "No, no, I'm not." Her brother kept saying stuff like that, and she was like, "You know what? It's fluid. There's a spectrum. There's a spectrum of attraction. I'm on the spectrum." Her brother started using it in classes. He was like, "My sister always says there's a spectrum."

In a lot of ways, Soraya's parents were permissive. They weren't the kind of people who stood on ceremony, but there were parts of their background that made them a little repressed. Talking about sex abstractly was okay, but talking about your own sexual behaviour felt not okay. Her mom seemed really open to her friends, but she wasn't Gloria Steinem. And even Gloria Steinem is a product of her time.

Soraya was really close to her mom. So much so that she found it difficult to separate herself from what her mother thought, or what she thought for her. She really didn't start separating her beliefs from her mother's until she was in her mid-thirties. There were things she maybe should have been questioning sooner.

Soraya wrote a piece for Longreads called "The Queer Generation Gap," which starts, "Should I be married to a woman? If today were yesterday, if all this sexual fluidity were in the discourse when I was coming of age in the '90s, would I have been with a woman instead of a man?" Soraya doesn't quite feel comfortable identifying as queer, or bisexual. She has a feeling that if she brought home a wife, then it somehow wouldn't be as ideal as if she brought home a husband. But she thinks that if she'd been born fifteen years later, she'd probably feel differently.

In the piece, she also wrote, "In my high school, no one was gay even if they were." Soraya feels like she—or maybe everyone—subconsciously knew that people were gay, but they couldn't admit it out loud. People couldn't even admit it to themselves. After high school, the moment someone came out, Soraya immediately realized she'd intuitively understood the person was queer. If she attended a school reunion and told people she was queer, her classmates would have the same reaction to her coming out. But she feels contrary about it. She doesn't want people to assume things about her. She'd probably say, "No! I'm not!"

In the article, Soraya writes about when younger white male celebrities play around with gender and sexuality. It doesn't always sit right with her. Someone like Ezra Miller acts flamboyant for a photo shoot, and he says in the corresponding interview, "I also sleep with men!" To Soraya, this comes across as performing things that are actually really important to other people. It feels maybe superficial, like these men are plugging into a trend, and for other people—older people, non-celebrities, non-white people—it's not a trend. It's their lives. White people, white men, get more space to play around.

But then, she also has another feeling: "Why can't I be like these kids?" It seems so easy for them. She gets this sense that she's somehow failed, and that's why she runs into these regressive edges of her personality. Soraya remembers a friend telling her about a woman around Soraya's age who'd come out in high school, and Soraya was like, *How the fuck did she do that? What kind of backbone did she have to have to do that?* As much as we would like to transcend the atmospheres in which we grow up, there's only so much we can do. At the end of the piece, when she addresses the younger generation with: "We're not mad at you. We're mad at ourselves," that's where that comes from. That feeling of, "Why am I constrained? Why can't I transcend these constraints?"

It's hard to grow up in an era when the standard is heterosexuality, and then break free of that idea. If you're the type of person who sort of judges someone when you first see them, and you've been trained to see everyone as straight, then you'll assume everyone is straight unless there's some kind of obvious indicator that they're gay. You think you have people down, but you're never quite right.

After Soraya's article about the queer generation gap came out, she heard from people who wondered why she was giving all these young men a hard time about their casual queerness, but she also heard from people around her age who understood where she was coming from. A gay man she went to high school with, who came out near the end of high school, or maybe right after, wrote to her and told her he felt similarly—surprised at the ease with which younger people came out and explored their genders and sexualities openly and publicly. To Soraya, it's the kind of complexity of feeling someone will get if they feel it and won't if they don't.

Even now, Soraya still wouldn't go around being like, "I'm queer." But she also feels like there aren't a lot of situations where people are like, "Hey, what are you?" Soraya doesn't necessarily conceive of herself as part of a queer conversation, but maybe that's an issue with the way she thinks of the conversation.

10

MOM, DAD, OTHER

ON AN AFTERNOON when we were a little more knee-deep in the after-effects of toddler tornado than usual, Will and I decided to put Sinclair, who was then seventeen months old, on the waitlist for a French-language preschool. Preschool would start when she was three.

When I looked up the preschool intake form and saw blank spaces only for *mère* and *père*, I let the tab languish, unattended, at the corner of my browser window. If I crossed out *mère*, I wasn't sure what I'd put in its place. I hadn't settled on a parent name. "Baba," which is probably the most common parental label used by non-binary people, means dad in multiple languages, and grandma in others; I didn't have a connection to it, and it felt culturally appropriative for me to borrow it. So I remained label-less.

At home, this didn't matter. Sinclair's first word, sometime between six and nine months, was "Boop!" At seventeen months, we were trying—

moderately unsuccessfully—to teach her to verbalize "yes" and "no." She preferred to say "cheese," "meow," and "uh-oh." When people asked us what parent names she used for us, we shrugged: we worked from home and were around her all the time. She hadn't bothered to call us anything yet. By then, I'd resigned myself to going by my first name with adults who would be interacting with her regularly—friends, family, teachers. Will was thinking he'd go by Dad; I wondered if this would cause some momentary misunderstandings because people would assume that I was Sinclair's dad's partner, and not her parent. But neither of us wanted to restrict Will's choice simply because there was nothing equivalent to Dad for me.

Labels are ubiquitous, contentious. The ones we're comfortable with slide by like water, so common that we don't even stop to think about them. It's only when we add new ones, or incorporate the unfamiliar, that labels begin to chafe. A comment on a piece about non-binary parenthood I co-wrote a few years ago sums up the hetero lament: "Don't you find all those labels divisive? Undermining? And reductive?" I really doubt that the person who wrote this stopped to wonder if calling their parents Mom and Dad was divisive, undermining, or reductive. Even if, perhaps, it was.

IN HETERO-PARENT FAMILIES, the words "Mom" and "Dad" generally delineate the roles each takes in the relationship, both with each other and with their kids. Although nothing is ever as simple as it appears, it remains true that for the majority of straight couples with kids, Mom handles the bulk of child care, housework, cooking, and household coordination, often while working; Dad works and pitches in with Mom's duties. This seems exhausting, a situation in which parenthood both erodes one's sense of self for many mothers and shores up outdated gender roles for both parents. We expect more of Mom, we're intensely critical of Mom, and to Dad we assign the condescending burden of lowered expectations. (In capsule form, thanks to Zoe Whittall: "I just want to be as universally revered by everyone as the man who holds his own baby in a coffee shop.")

When you're a queer parent, there is no automatic delineation of roles; every family looks a little different, but somebody has to bathe the child, teach her to read, do the laundry. There's no falling back on cultural expectations, so a negotiation follows: What's important to you? What do you like, dislike? How will we share things in a way that seems fair and sustainable? For my partner and me, this negotiation extends from things that are more minor—I never vacuum and he rarely cooks dinner—to those that feel more meaningful. Our kid carries my last name, for example. And another of her first words was "butt," indicative of the fact that my partner has been her primary nine-to-five caregiver—I would have taught her, if I were changing the lion's share of diapers, to say "bum."

It feels surreal to be comfortable tackling the gendered expectations of parenthood but to have no warm, loving way to voice who you are to your own child. Non-binary folks have adopted pronouns like they and ze, to carve out space for ourselves in language. Parenting labels could use a similar revision—to establish terms that are recognized not only in queer communities but also more broadly in our culture.

I've learned you are the best parent to your kid when you take time to triage your own needs and wants alongside theirs. When I was pregnant in Montreal, I thought, for the sake of not appearing too "weird" or "difficult," that I could stomach nine months of *maman* and *madame* from medical professionals before returning to my real self. It's worth noting that after Sinclair was born there was no change in gender presentation for me—I'm masculine-of-centre but often read, I think, as a queer or butch woman—but rather a return to being more assertive about pronouns, honorifics, titles, and the assumptions people make about my family structure.

But then, it wasn't that simple: as the parent of a young kid, your "real self" is more often than not necessarily tethered to your relationship with your child and the way that relationship is read in the world.

ON THE FERRY FROM HORSESHOE BAY in West Vancouver to Langdale on the Sunshine Coast, I often walk up and down the aisles with Sinclair, who likes to stop and make new friends. It is bewildering the number of grown adults who talk to her, referring to me, in the third person, as Mom. Since I am the same person who often receives a quick gender-check on my way into the women's bathroom on those same ferries, my guess is that this happens to me now for the same reason it happened when I was pregnant: pregnancy and child care are seen as inherently feminine acts, most often associated with women. Being spoken about in the third person while I was immediately present was not something that occurred to me nearly as often pre-parenthood. I've considered buying "they/she" pins (I'm comfortable with both pronouns) and carpeting my body with them, but I don't know if it would help. Maybe a "Not the mama" iron-on?

The experience of being misgendered in this way comes with the added weight of feminism, despite its best efforts, having managed to undermine less the idea of "motherhood" than it has something like "woman." While feminism has tried to move the needle on gendered divisions of labour in parenting, we are still culturally stuck in 101-level conversations about mothering and fathering—school pickups, caregiving, household management. "Motherhood" is a field that has not expanded nearly as much as "woman." Because I present as masculine, I don't deal with garden-variety sexism—catcalls, assumptions about work-related competency, sexual harassment—nearly as often as feminine women. Having a kid, though, has undermined that, reinscribing both a womanhood that doesn't suit me and the corresponding binaristic ideas we hold about parenting.

Case in point: another common refrain, when I travel alone and a stranger learns that I have a toddler, is "Who's taking care of her?!" Once, an older man followed up with "You trust him to do that?" When people call me Mom, I dissociate for a moment before returning to my well-worn body. But when they ask me what I've done with my child in order to travel away from her, I leave an accidental long pause, unable to get to the premise of the question nearly quickly enough.

Gender was also something we considered when it came time to choose Sinclair's name; before we even conceived, we'd narrowed our list to names that could work for a girl, boy, or non-binary kid. In raising her, we're hopefully creating the circumstances where she'll feel free to be herself. But it's conversations like the ones we have ad nauseam while travelling and in other public spaces that led us to choose the path of least resistance when it came to her pronouns—statistically, she's more likely to align with the gender she was assigned at birth, and I know from personal experience that "they" is still somewhat of a social burden to carry, one I wouldn't feel comfortable imposing. We'll change to suit Sinclair's needs if and when she shares a different preference.

The year after Sinclair was born, people wished me a happy Mother's Day, and a little piece of me felt like it had been hole-punched out. My loved ones weren't being harmful on purpose, but it actually felt worse than when a stranger misgendered me: I wondered if I wasn't legibly trans enough, if I hadn't made myself known, if I could correct someone I cared for deeply for the twenty-fourth time without causing harm to our relationship. I wondered how people thought about me, talked about me, when I wasn't around. (Was my request for gender-neutral kinship terms seen as something quirky, rather than something foundational?)

It hurts, but I recognize that it's a problem that's both interpersonal and cultural—it wouldn't be as hard for friends and family to conceive of me correctly if they'd grown up in a place that made space for me. In a place that had a parental term for me, like it has for most people. I deeply hope that all the recent mainstream discussions about trans identities and queer identities has brought some understanding, some shift that will make it easier for the generations of queer parents who follow us.

THANKFULLY, THE ACTUAL EXPERIENCE of being a non-binary parent to my child is worlds apart from my interactions with others as a parent. My kid cares about being loved, about snacking, about going outside, about reading books. I love her, I give her snacks, we go outside, I read her books. And when I asked my partner if he'd be a different dad if it wasn't for me—if he'd ended up with a woman, someone comfortable with mothering—he said no. The whole point of having a kid, he said, is to raise her.

I'm not sure if I am queering parenthood just by being a parent. I guess I am if I'll be asking my kid's schools to edit their intake forms so that there's a space for me to put my name, to render myself a bureaucratic part of her world on top of being a daily cornerstone of it. There are days when I don't think about the ways in which being non-binary and being a parent intersect, mesh, and clash, when my top priorities include picking all the fish-shaped cheese crackers off the floor and making sure the toddler doesn't do a header off a kitchen chair. And then there are others when my internal monologue is the Manifesto of the Happily Boring Queer Parent: I need the world to make just enough space for me that I can become completely unremarkable.

laura

LAURA IS THIRTY-THREE. She grew up in Steinbach, Manitoba. It was the Prairies: everything was flat, there was a lot of sky, and it all felt very wide open. The nearest city was Winnipeg, an hour away, and even though Steinbach was surrounded by even smaller towns and villages, it felt self-contained. It seemed to exist apart from everything else, not following the progression of other towns to get more modern. Steinbach wasn't the smallest town, but it was pretty conservative and small-minded.

Laura didn't conceptualize of herself as queer until a bit later in life. As a kid, she felt artistic. She thought the world was big, in a way that her parents didn't. They couldn't see eye to eye. Laura's experience of Steinbach was that her family, and other good Christian Mennonite families, would go to church. For a lot of teenagers, it seemed like rebelling and not going to church was a phase, a way to assert yourself in a typical teenage way, where you're figuring out your life and how your beliefs are going to look as an adult. That's something Laura got from older peers who grew up with religious backgrounds. But then they came back to organized religion. It wasn't the same for Laura. Her parents' church was the lens through which she saw things that were wrong in Steinbach.

Laura only realized after leaving Steinbach that part of the problem is that it's a well-to-do town. People at her church always seemed to have more money than her family. They were part of an Evangelical Mennonite Conference congregation where it seemed as though wealth was considered a symbol of your being a good Christian. It was only later that she realized that a lot of the Mennonite communities in Winnipeg purposely try to live in a more earth-conscious, socially conscious way. The perspective of Laura's church really rubbed her the wrong way as a kid, but without any comparison, she had a hard time figuring out why.

Laura's family was very conservative and quite religious when she and her brother were growing up. There were a lot of TV shows she couldn't watch. One of Laura's best friends in high school was gay. Laura's mother would say stuff to her like, "I can like him. I just don't have to like what he does." That old chestnut.

Her family has changed completely in the last ten years. Her brother got married about seven years ago, and then he got abruptly divorced a couple years into his marriage. Laura's parents also divorced about a year after her brother got married. Even after that, Laura's dad thought that Laura dating women was not going to be something that they talked about. And he made Laura's brother and Laura's sister-in-law feel bad that they'd lived together before they got married. Throughout his divorce, Laura's brother was a bit more open than usual—he's a fairly private guy. Her brother's divorce, and going through his own divorce, eventually changed her dad.

Laura feels like she's culturally about twenty years ahead of her parents. Her mom has acknowledged this. There were a lot of situations where Laura was like, "Um, this isn't healthy," or "This isn't productive for me," or "I think this is straight-up wrong." And then fifteen to twenty years later, her parents were like, "Oh, she was on to something."

When she goes back to Steinbach now, it feels like her parents' town. She goes there to see her dad or her grandma, and that's about it. If she has to go to a store, or see people, it can feel quite strange. Because inevitably she sees folks that she remembers going to high school with, and everyone has a child. But she feels fairly vehemently that she's not going to have kids, and she's probably not going to partner up. When you live in a small town, it feels like that's the only thing you can do. If there was just a little bit more ability to become a person enough to realize that you might not want that, there might be more variation. There could be single people there, single people in their thirties. The thing about religious small towns is that you have to get married to have sex.

That being said, no one in Laura's immediate family is religious anymore. Her dad stopped going to church when her mom left, because he didn't want to go by himself. And then everything else sort of relaxed. Leaving the church, Laura thinks, enabled her family to take a more clear-eyed look at a lot of things.

Laura doesn't date a lot. She had her first serious relationship a few years after she went through a serious self-reckoning, a self-coming-out. When she was having her coming-out moment, there was no significant other attached. So in some ways, that laid the groundwork so that when she was dating someone she didn't have that strong anger, that self-conviction, like "This is who I am!" When it came to her relationship with her parents, the earlier single self paved the way for the later coupled self.

When Laura first moved to Winnipeg from Steinbach, it was a very lonely time in her life. It took ages for her to start hanging out with people. She would go to her classes and go home in between them. She's introverted and moderately anti-social, so she wasn't sure how many friends she wanted. She didn't really take things very seriously in her first year, but after that she decided she had to stick to her studies. One of the next classes she took was Women's and Gender Studies, and that sort of opened everything up. She graduated with a major in English and a minor in gender studies.

Laura was always motivated to do well in school, but what she learned from books always felt at odds with what she was being taught in school and at church and at home. Going to university really undid all of those teachings. Books are about opening your world up, and life in Steinbach was about keeping your world closed.

Going to university opened up a whole world for Laura. She came out to her mom by phoning her in the middle of the night, when she was walking home drunk from a bar. Even today Laura doesn't quite understand why she phoned her in the dead of night. Laura has no idea exactly what she said. She doesn't know if she said, "I'm a lesbian," or "I'm not straight." Her mom cried, but she also said, "I knew." This happened near the end of her parents living together. Laura's dad woke up because her mom was on the phone, and then her mom just told him. In hindsight, it's a bit embarrassing. Maybe she had to be drunk to come out to them.

Today, Laura's mom would call herself liberal, and could claim some familiarity with gay people and issues, but that was a journey. When Laura came out, her parents had some difficulty with it. Looking back, she thinks they were just worried for her. Laura also has a chronic illness. Her parents had been worried for her from the time she was a kid, and then it was like, "Oh, another thing."

Being queer then was not zeitgeisty, like it can feel now. It was a risk to talk about going to the gay bar. This would have been in, maybe, 2007. Laura remembers talking to her cousins about it, and her cousins being a bit closed-minded. It feels a bit weird that certain members of her family now pick up on aspects of queer culture that are in the mainstream. They get to feel like they're part of something—but when Laura was younger she was legitimately scared. She definitely feels like she's part of a middle generation of queer people, coming out just before things really started to change.

11

MILK AND GENERATIVENESS

SINCLAIR WAS BORN HUNGRY. Small and blue and hungry. A few hours after
the C-section I was narcoleptic from the epidural, and as she tried to latch
and drink, I couldn't stop falling asleep. "Whoa," Will said, or something
like it, and he held the baby onto me. She was born determined, and that
determination stayed with her as she grew from tiny to small to a little bit
bigger.

After we returned home to our one-bedroom apartment on the third
floor of a triplex in Little Italy in Montreal, I got to know her a little better.
I witnessed the look of concentration overtake her face as she zeroed in
for milk. She latched easily. She drank quickly. She handily mastered the
skill of breathing through her nose.

When I worked at Tim Hortons in the early 2000s, the milk and cream
came in ten-litre sacs with built-in spouts. The sacs were rectangular, made
of clear plastic, slick with condensation. They were heavy, difficult enough

to carry from the fridge to the front of the store that the only real way to do it was to hug the sac against your chest. The whole rest of the day after replacing the cream or milk, I'd smell waves of soured dairy emanating from my striped polycotton blend shirt. This smell returned a few days after Sinclair was born.

ANNE THÉRIAULT, A FEMINIST WRITER, once shared an illustration on Twitter that she'd drawn of breastfeeding. The caption explained that it was what breastfeeding felt like for her; the illustration depicted delicate purple blooms at the ends of milk ducts, leading out towards the nipple, where they entered the mouth of the baby, bursting into pink and yellow-purple, orange and red and blue flowers.

It is a glowing and kind and practical way to view a breastfeeding bond. Will's mom said once, when Sinclair was about six months old, that she'd grown so big and large, she'd gone from newborn to a whole little human crawling across the kitchen floor, by drinking my milk alone. It wasn't something I'd considered, not in that way. I'd felt wonder at houseplants growing on nothing more than sunlight and water but hadn't mustered the same wonder for myself, or for Sinclair, at least not as it related to her consumption of my milk. To Thériault, to Will's mom, breastfeeding was a generative, near-magical act. To me, if felt much more complex—something that I participated in directly, even as I felt like somewhat of an outsider.

IN MY EARLY TWENTIES, I went to a Guelph General Hospital auxiliary build-ing for a breast reduction consultation. The plastic surgeon's office was in a squat three- or four-storey building, and I took the stairs up to his office, which was decorated in taupes and oranges and browns. I'd had my wisdom teeth removed in an office like it (after administering laughing gas, the dentist had said, "You'll know it's working when the geese in the paintings on the wall start to flap their wings"), and the surgeon's office was comfortably similar.

The surgeon didn't give me enough time to take my shirt off before he came back into the room. He knocked and entered all in one go. I covered my torso with my arms, expecting him to give me a minute, but he pressed farther into the room. He appraised my breasts: lifted them, palpated them. I could see him visualizing the transformation. Using a marker, he drew a circle around my nipple and a line down the centre of the bottom half of my breast, and then a semicircle at the base. If I went through with the surgery, these were the cuts he'd make. He'd remove my nipples and then put them back on. I might lose sensation. I might lose the ability to breastfeed.

In his office after the physical exam, the surgeon posed a series of questions. "When did you know your breasts were too large?" he asked. I thought, They are too large for me. I thought of another person inhabiting my body and being fine with them. I pictured my already developing nine-year-old self and felt protective of her. He asked when I realized my breasts were bigger than everyone else's. I began to dissociate. Part of my consciousness floated above me, observing. The self who was answering was a simulacrum. I'd gone stiff. The ever-present tension in my mid-to-upper back—a side effect of having large breasts when I'd never even wanted small ones—got louder, drowning everything else out.

I left the surgeon's office knowing I'd never let him touch me again. I put off the idea of a breast reduction in part so that I could pretend, for a while, that the consultation had never happened. I did think about having a kid, probably just one. If I stayed with my then-partner, I thought, I'd be the one gestating the kid. Maybe it was selfish to want something for myself that would exclude the possibility that I would be able to give of myself to someone else. I would never exact that pressure on someone else, anyone else, but maybe when it came to me, the idea that breast was best had permeated my consciousness to such an extent that in addition to feeling violated by the interaction, I also began to feel chastened, self-centred, vain.

IN ELEMENTARY SCHOOL, my class put on a production of *The Tale of Peter Rabbit*. I wanted to be Peter. Instead, I was cast, alongside a girl named Maggie, who was good at golf, as a plump robin. "Run, Peter, Run!" we sang. "Run, Peter, Run!" I'd wanted to be the small, swift, mischievous rabbit. The music teacher praised our high notes.

One morning, on my way into Vancouver from Surrey, after Will and Sinclair and I moved back out to the West Coast and in with Will's mom for a spell, it was grey and rainy as I was walking to the bus. Grey and rainy, just like the morning before it. I had switched from feeding Sinclair milk directly from the breast most of the time to pumping it while I was at work. I was exhausted.

Walking to the bus, I saw the hare I saw often on cloudy days—eating grass on a strip next to the sidewalk, bordered by a low wooden barrier and, beyond it, blackberries and brush. The hare and the baby both seemed so vulnerable, and so perfect, reminding me of the importance of tenderness and carefulness and care. What would it look like, I thought, if I applied that tenderness and carefulness and care to myself?

I had no answer and several answers at once: *go back to sleep, work from home, get some exercise, go to the dentist. Get a breast reduction.*

FROM A TRANS MALE DISCUSSION GROUP I learned that people whose BMIs fall in the obese range are sometimes denied top surgery, and that people whose BMIs are considered overweight are sometimes required to pay more for surgery. I haven't weighed myself in years (I turned away from the scale while pregnant), but I'd guess I would be required to lose twenty, or maybe thirty, pounds to drop from "overweight" to "normal." I am unconvinced about normal. When I was ill, about ten years ago now, and my weight dropped, I was still in the normal range when I stopped menstruating. Normal when I became so anemic my doctor told me I'd need a blood transfusion.

The BMI is "unscientific bullshit," a friend of mine says. But I don't want to have to wait, again, for surgery. Even before my first consultation, in my teens, my family doctor told me to try losing weight, which could bring me down a cup size, before I considered surgery. I left her office shamed but knowing that losing weight wouldn't give me what I wanted, which was to have no breasts at all; later, when I was temporarily thin and still had large breasts, I felt vindicated. I still wanted surgery—or rather, I still wanted to not have breasts. The desire was a steady thrum under every other thing I did, every other thought I had.

When I think about promoting this book—when I think of standing on a stage and embodying the words in this book—I don't want to do it with breasts. I'm not sure I can do it in this iteration of my body. I don't know if I can get close enough to what is "normal"—when I see "normal"

I think perfect, I think ideal, I think *eludes me*. I don't know if I will be judged worthy for surgery.

WHEN I WORKED AT *Adbusters* I was also editing news columns for *This Magazine*. A trans dad, Trevor MacDonald, pitched a column talking about chestfeeding and his involvement with La Leche League. MacDonald, who'd had top surgery and chestfed with the aid of a supplemental feeding tube and donor milk to bolster his own milk, had relied in part on La Leche to help him through difficulties lactating and feeding his baby. Later, when he applied to become a group leader, to pay forward the support he'd received from others, his application was denied. "The roles of mothers and fathers are not interchangeable," a spokesperson for La Leche League wrote in a letter to MacDonald. "Since an LLLC Leader is a mother who has breastfed a baby, a man cannot become an LLLC Leader."

In Surrey, a friend sent me an article from the *Stranger* about breast milk; she wrote something like, "This is cool! It may or may not be a fit for your experiences." The article opens, "To produce breast milk, mothers literally melt their own body fat ... we literally dissolve parts of ourselves, starting with gluteal-femoral fat, aka our butts, and turn it into liquid to feed our babies." The author is a food writer who is interested in the science of food—in this case, breast milk. How breastfed babies get fewer colds. How the food a breastfeeding parent eats is transmitted, in part, through breast milk, giving a baby their first shot at palate development. The article is also in part a salvo for the development of paid maternity leave in the United States, a thing we have in Canada but that many Canadians—those cobbling together part-time jobs, contracting, freelancing—may not have access to. The article doesn't acknowledge that anyone but mothers breastfeed, and reading it as a breastfeeding parent who'd fall into the category of people the salvo is meant to support—those lacking the resources to not work for a while—made me feel like I was perhaps a bit of a charity case, one that everyone I could have allied with had temporarily, or permanently, forgotten.

AS I RAN INTO MY OWN BREASTFEEDING DIFFICULTIES—mostly, keeping my supply up while I was away from home for eleven hours a day—I looked up tools and techniques and resources for how best to keep my kid fed, and I felt, as a non-binary person, like I was standing a ways back from a circle of chairs, observing a meeting in progress. Women bleed, women carry, women feed. I bleed, I carry, I feed. I am not a woman.

I read "breast milk is much more than food: It's potent medicine and, simultaneously, a powerful medium of communication between mothers and their babies," and performed a simultaneous translation: *a powerful medium of communication between lactating parents and their babies.* By acknowledging an adjacency to masculinity have I ceded my right to inclusion? Or by lactating have I ceded a right to my gender?

What would it mean to celebrate the particularly feminine contribution of breastfeeding while also celebrating everyone who breastfeeds and isn't a woman?

I can imagine what Anne Thériault means when she draws the life-giving connection between herself and her child. I like, in particular, that the flowers she used to depict milk ducts were one colour, and the flowers depicting the effects of milk in the feeding baby were a burst of diverse blooms. I liked to witness the amazement Will's mom had when she looked at Sinclair and thought of the milk that sustained her—maybe she was thinking of what it had been like to have and to feed her own kids. I like that both Thériault and Will's mom feel what they feel, but I don't feel it, not really. Breastfeeding feels complicated to me. A way to rehabilitate, in part, the complex relationship I have with my complex body. I have focused on the nuts and bolts of milk production and child growth, isolating the practice for its practical elements, without being able to make space for the emotive part, the connective part, the part that acknowledges the way I love and care for Sinclair.

I am thinking about the generative act of nursing, the generative act of my nursing, the time I put in, my closeness with Sinclair. I am also thinking of the generative act of Will feeding Sinclair with the bottle of milk that I pumped. As Will feeds Sinclair, he, too, is communicating with her. She lies in the crook of his arm and he tilts the bottle back for her and the room goes quiet except for the sound of her drinking. It is a moment that requires Will to gauge how hungry she is, how hungry she will be. He has honed the art of warming the milk to the temperature she prefers; she is impatient as he gets the bottle ready but won't take it if the milk is too cold. When she's done, she sits up, and Will responds by setting the bottle aside. As she grows older, Sinclair opts to do many things for herself. But even as she can hold her own bottle, she chooses not to. She prefers to have Will, or me, hold it for her.

I am thinking about ways to talk about milk and parenthood that hold a place for women (trans and cis), non-binary parents, and trans dads. For people who can't, or don't want to, nurse.

I AM BUOYED, researching this essay eight years after I edited his column, to learn that Trevor MacDonald did eventually join La Leche League as a leader, that in fact he helped develop the league's messaging and outreach to trans and non-binary parents, which includes notes that gender dysphoria may preclude breast- or chestfeeding, that it's okay to prioritize one's mental health, that some parents with dysphoria choose to pump and bottle-feed, and others use donor milk—essentially, that there is no one way to do things correctly.

I am able to talk about everything I talk about in this essay, and more broadly in this book, because of the work of my trans forebears, some of whom are my age, or not much older.

I AM NOT SURE IF I WOULD HAVE MADE THE SAME DECISION, or a different one, if I'd first sought surgery in a more welcoming, less oppressive environment. I am not sure if surgery will fix the way I feel about my body—the physical pain, the social discomfort, the semi-estrangement from my own breasts. But I don't think that gender-affirming surgeries need to be a panacea for trans people in order for trans people to have access to them. And even if it doesn't solve everything, I still want surgery.

I do think that I will feel relieved, like the pressure on my jaw that let up after having my wisdom teeth out, once I am breast-free. But I've had enough other unrelated surgeries to know that there is often a longer period of healing than you might expect, and that perfection doesn't exist. I may have the surgery and initially feel disappointed; I will have waited for that moment for more than two decades, and it is hard for something you've imagined so many times to live up to your expectations. But it's also possible that I'll remove my bandages, put on a T-shirt, and feel for the first time, without the use of a constrictive binder, a sense of gender euphoria. The sense that I have, for once, prioritized providing myself with tenderness and care. I am not sure what bounty surgery will bring me. I am sure that it won't result directly in being misgendered less; only social change, the same type that would remind journalists and public health officials and doctors to include some language about chestfeeding, about trans and non-binary gestational parents, will do that.

What I can predict—it took writing this essay for me to figure it out—is that I will be able to feel grateful that I nursed Sinclair only after I've had surgery. That I'll be able to look back and feel grateful to myself, to fully recognize what it meant, only after I am allowed to fully recognize myself.

nadine

NADINE IS THIRTY-ONE. She's a lesbian and non-binary and queer. She grew up in Gimli, Manitoba, about an hour north of Winnipeg, next to Lake Winnipeg. It's known as the capital of New Iceland because it's got the second-biggest population of Icelandic people outside of Iceland. Nadine's maternal great-grandfather was one of the earliest settlers from Iceland. The area was very white. There were five churches. In the summertime, tourists came from everywhere, and the population swelled from about 3,000 to 10,000.

Gimli is a fishing town. Nadine's grandpa, four of her uncles, and a few of their partners all fish. There was always pickerel being filleted on the counter. Her grandpa was always drying fish to make harðfiskur, which is a dried, salted fish people would hang out on their porches. It was normal to have stinky fish everywhere. Nadine loves it, actually. When she went to

Iceland for a few days for her honeymoon, she bought some and left it in her hotel room and her partner was not impressed.

Nadine's mom raised her. Her mom left her dad when Nadine was born. She was born up north, in a place called The Pas, where her father was in the RCMP, and her mom moved back to Gimli when she left him. Nadine thought it was pretty rad to be raised by a single mom, but it probably wasn't the most fun for her mother. She was an RCMP officer too, so Nadine was a latchkey kid for a lot of her childhood.

Nadine has an older half sister, but she didn't know about her growing up. She was raised as an only child, the eldest of twenty-seven cousins. Her mom is one of seven siblings. Even though she was an only child, she always had family to go visit. It felt like there were a lot of shitty dads and a lot of great moms who took care of everyone, so the cousins would hop between houses. Not Nadine's house, though, because her mom had to work all the time.

Nadine and her mom lived in Winnipeg Beach, which is just outside of Gimli. She lived in the middle of nowhere. A lot of people in Vancouver, where Nadine lives now, don't know how to drive. If you grow up in a small town and you don't know how to drive, you're not going anywhere.

Their house was small, on an acre lot. It was about a fifteen-minute walk from the lake, and it was just flat. Flat, flat, flat. Absolute prairie big sky. It was easy to run into the bush with friends, get drunk in the woods. There was a weird class hierarchy between the Beachers and the townies. Nadine remembers her mom saw one of the Winnipeg Beach teachers smack a kid once, and she was like, "Nope, you're not going there." So she went to school in town instead.

Nadine remembers always feeling different, but she didn't associate it with queerness for a long time. She's always lived mostly in her head, and she felt isolated in Gimli, but mostly didn't mind it. Even when she got bullied in high school, she still managed to have some pretty good friendships. In hindsight, all the gay kids became friends, even the ones who didn't know yet that they were gay or trans. It's funny to see how that works out.

Nadine can't remember the precise moment when she learned what gay was. She can't trace when she was told explicitly that being gay was bad, or was something we don't talk about, but she remembers having that feeling. She never remembers her mom saying anything explicitly homophobic. She was still homophobic, though—everyone is, a little bit, when you are living in a heterosexual culture. Nadine remembers the first time she fooled around with some of her girlfriends, when she was drunk at fourteen. They almost had sex. And the next day, Nadine felt really over-whelmed. She threw up, and she ended up going over to her aunt's and melting down. Just repeating to herself, "I'm not gay, I'm not gay," which, looking back, she's really saying, "Oh, honey, you're gay."

When Nadine was fourteen, she used to play a game with her mom where she'd be like, "Would you love me if?" "Would you love me if I was a ditchdigger? Would you love me if I murdered someone? Would you love me if I was gay?" Silence. "Yes, of course." And then she'd move onto the next thing. She would reach out, blab, freak out, and go back.

What complicated things was that Nadine was in and out of crisis centres between fifteen and nineteen, because she was so depressed. She got bullied for having tried to kill herself at fifteen. In that way, she's glad she got to be just the crazy kid, instead of the crazy dyke. Her narrative was always very much like, I'm going to get out of this small town, because I'm smarter than all of these people. And I don't care if I'm crazy. I don't care if I'm ugly. In hindsight, she had some very not-feminist thoughts, like, They're all going to just stay here and have kids. The kinds of stories we tell ourselves to get through shitty things. Nadine romanticized her own difference, a bit, as a survival strategy.

One of the friends Nadine had made out with developed feelings for her, and wasn't in a terribly stable mental place. Nadine told her she wasn't gay and that she needed to give her some space. She didn't know how to say, "I'm gay, but I'm not gay for you." She's always felt a little guilty about that.

Nadine moved to Winnipeg when she was seventeen to go to university. She did a seven-year undergrad. For a lot of that period, she was dating a super abusive guy. She dumped him when she was twenty-one, and then she dated one nice guy, and then she came out as a big roaring dyke when she was twenty-three. She shaved her head and deliberately gained thirty pounds. It was fun. She gravitated towards the women's centre, the women's studies department, and the LGBT centre.

The most typical fanfare kind of coming-out came when she was twenty-three. Nadine was dating a friend of hers, who was transitioning, whom she'd met in the women's studies department when she was nineteen. They'd been roommates, and they started dating long-distance. Before that, Nadine cheated on her shitty boyfriend with a lot of women. She had a weird sense of tacit knowing, denial. But then on her twenty-third birthday, she told her mom and stepdad, sat them down, essentially. She sat down her aunt and her cousins, too.

Now, it's hard to disassociate the small town where she grew up from all of her most unhappy years, when she was so mentally ill, when she was suicidal. She doesn't like seeing people she knew, because most of them don't recognize her. Gender-wise, she looks so completely different now. When she takes her wife back—her wife looks just like a feminine boy—that always attracts the worst kind of scary, white, redneck attention. When they go, they don't stray far from Nadine's parents' house.

At the same time, Nadine's PhD research focuses on postwar social history, and she's really into the history of sexuality, LGBT studies. Her primary method is oral history, because she finds that people's stories are a lot more interesting than anything you can put together in an academic text. She finds people's memories to be most historically important, and they're often, too, what ends up getting relegated to the margins. So she's writing about LGBTQ-, queer-, trans-, Two-Spirit-identified folks who have lived and been a part of some sort of political organizing in rural BC, from 1965 to now. She's talking to people who were born in small places and moved to cities, people who stayed, people who returned. She's trying to interrogate the static narrative of: you grow up in a small rural town, which tends to be homophobic, and then in order to move through this proverbial—but also material—closet, you move from a small town to a city.

Because she grew up in rural Manitoba, where it was super homophobic, her trajectory was absolutely that. And that's definitely a lot of people's experience. But Nadine thinks that it's also a limited perspective. And it makes rurality seem like a static thing, and like something that is the antithesis of how we conceive of queerness. This perspective ends up participating in erasure. Doing interviews with older lesbian activists for her master's degree, Nadine found that many women had stories about rural dyke areas and the informal communities people had created. There's been a lot of activism in places that people don't necessarily associate with activism.

It's been interesting for Nadine to confront her own sense of "Fuck no, I will never live in a small town again." On the one hand, that sense of urgency she had about leaving her small town has diminished. But on the other hand, even almost twenty years later, it was so bad that she's still kind of like, "Eh, I don't know."

12

THE PEOPLE'S POETRY

some unthinking god
is made of towering flowers; his eye
in the tall blue tulip sky,
a profound petal there; I arrest its blooming.

I want the flowers beheaded,
the garden sink,
the rain deny its claim to princedom there
—GWENDOLYN MACEWEN, "CERTAIN FLOWERS"

IN THE EARLY 1960S, a part-bar, part-coffee shop, part-venue space opened on St. Nicholas Street, a few blocks up from Yonge and Wellesley in Toronto. Soon after it opened, poet Milton Acorn, then in his late thirties, began to hold court there. The Bohemian Embassy held poetry readings on Thursday nights, when Acorn would read, generally overstaying his welcome on the stage. Afterwards, he would find himself surrounded by younger poets. Margaret Atwood, then a student at the University of Toronto, read at the Embassy; a little later, a teenage Gwendolyn MacEwen found the spot, the community—and Acorn.

Acorn was bombastic, drank a lot, often had a fat cigar sticking out from the side of his mouth. MacEwen was slight and half his age but had a compelling voice of her own. Unlike many of her contemporaries, she wasn't at university. She was self-taught; she'd had a tumultuous— occasionally violent, marked by alcoholism and mental illness—home life. Many of the books that chronicle Acorn and MacEwen's relationship come close to saying that Acorn was something of a father figure for the younger poets gathered at the Embassy—dispensing poetic advice, maybe acting more like a big brother. Acorn started off as MacEwen's "poetic mentor," but their relationship soon morphed, and they began to date. Eventually, they married. This was something Acorn wanted and MacEwen initially did not; he'd proposed in December 1960, when she was nineteen and he was thirty-seven, and she'd said no, writing, "Milt, my love is not the same as yours ... I feel no need to find myself physically, sensually, emotionally in another person ... I'm still getting acquainted with life, with myself." However, she agreed to his proposal a little later; he was in Prince Edward Island for the winter, and she was missing him while he was away.

Acorn and MacEwen's friends speculated about why they had gotten together at all. Chris Gudgeon's biography of Milton Acorn, Out of This World, says people referred to them as Beauty and the Beast. It was easy to see why Acorn was drawn to MacEwen—she was young, beautiful, talented, and insecure. MacEwen, Gudgeon writes, "fed Milt's lopsided vision of himself as a heroic poet-knight, battling the dragons of injustice, and leaving the fair maidens swooning." (Another Acorn biographer, Richard Lemm, is more explicit: "He had a constant companion who would listen to his political discourses. A sexually experienced man, he could teach and savour his less experienced lover.") Although it was less clear what had drawn MacEwen to Acorn, one friend from the Embassy pointed out that when they met, in contrast to later on, Acorn seemed confident, strong, clean-shaven, eccentric but put-together. Acorn and MacEwen had friends who guessed that part of the reason she was attracted to him was career-related—she was "ambitious" and saw him as "established," a way to further her writing and publishing goals; Al Purdy thought "Gwen was with Milton because Milton was 'getting attention.'"

Rosemary Sullivan, MacEwen's biographer, writes that it's important to be careful about the way we think about MacEwen and Acorn's relationship in retrospect. There was a power imbalance, and the relationship seemed doomed from the start, and Acorn was persistent, but there's no evidence that he was abusive, either physically or emotionally. At least, not until the relationship crumbled. MacEwen took a solo trip to Israel a few months after her wedding; when she returned, the distance and solitude had given her a new perspective on Toronto, and her relationship. As Sullivan puts it in Shadow Maker, "Almost as soon as she had married, Gwendolyn recognized that she had made a terrible mistake." MacEwen wanted a marriage of equals, and Acorn wanted a wife. Acorn was "deeply conservative" at heart, homophobic, anti-abortion (he wrote at least one terrible poem about it), and he wanted to see "supper on the table every night."

MacEwen and Acorn had an open marriage; he'd taken advantage of this when she was away, and she began a side relationship with a painter when she returned from Israel. Acorn gave her an ultimatum—him or the painter—and, not even a year into their marriage, she chose to leave. It was a choice that Acorn could not brook. He fell apart. He drank, showing up on friends' doorsteps in the middle of the night, distraught and drunk. He wrote MacEwen angry, bitter letters. ("One letter from that time begins with 'You Dirty Bitch' and ends up asking, 'WHERE IN THE WORLD DID YOU LEARN TO BE SUCH A LOUSE?'" writes Gudgeon; another, quoted in Shadow Maker, sent after MacEwen told Acorn of her intentions to divorce him, "accus[es] her of being 'the Great North American Castrator.'") MacEwen wrote back, at least at the beginning, explaining herself, trying to make him understand. Reading the snippets of his letters that are included in their biographies, it appears as though Acorn's life had gone to pieces, and he'd set the blame squarely on the shoulders of his much younger ex, who simply wanted space, freedom, and an amicable divorce. When Acorn refused to give her one—it was the era before no-fault divorces—MacEwen was forced to travel across the country, to Vancouver, to gather evidence of his marital infidelity in order to petition the courts. Purdy, who'd been Acorn's best man at the wedding, reluctantly acted as a witness to Acorn's adultery so that MacEwen could finally break free of the marriage.

In 1969, years later, MacEwen and Acorn were both announced finalists, alongside George Bowering, for the Governor General's Literary Award for Poetry or Drama. Acorn was still a mess—outstaying his welcome at friends' houses, drinking, not bathing, suicidal, hospitalized for depression, still half hoping MacEwen might come back and blaming her for everything that was wrong in his life. When MacEwen found out her book *The Shadow-Maker* was shortlisted alongside Acorn's *I've Tasted My Blood*, Nick Mount writes in his book *Arrival: The Story of CanLit*, "She was afraid enough of him to write to the judges that if there was any chance of her having to share the award with Acorn, she would rather withdraw her book from consideration." But she and Bowering won, sharing the award, and Acorn didn't.

CanLit did not graciously accept MacEwen and Bowering's win. Instead, poets Irving Layton and Eli Mandel co-authored an open letter protesting Acorn's loss. The letter was in part a call for money, to be raised and "presented to Milton Acorn as the Canadian Poet's Award." Another public plea for Acorn, this time an editorial by poets Seymour Mayne and Kenneth Hertz in a now-defunct Montreal literary magazine, reads, "Either because of literary politics or a gross ignorance of Canadian poetry on the part of the Canada Council jury, Milton Acorn has been denied the Governor General's Award that he truly has earned." Acorn's supporters generally focused their ire at Bowering. One of the three jurors who'd chosen MacEwen's and Bowering's books over Acorn's was Warren Tallman, an American who'd been hired to teach English at the University of British Columbia; the thinking went that Bowering's style, which was influenced by US poets, was emblematic of a type of cultural imperialism that needed to be studiously avoided if CanLit was to be its own proper national cultural project.

Five days after MacEwen and Bowering were feted at their awards ceremony in Ottawa, a broad swath of CanLit figures, including Layton, Purdy, and Atwood, showed up at Grossman's Tavern on Spadina Avenue in Toronto to witness Acorn receiving a cheque for $1,000 and a medallion naming him the People's Poet. When I think of this night—Acorn got so drunk he lost his prize cheque twice, his friends let him read for forty minutes, he was roundly celebrated—I immediately picture MacEwen and wonder how she felt, if she was at home in her small apartment that night, if there was anyone with her. And I wonder if anyone at Grossman's thought about MacEwen. Did they wonder, celebrating Acorn, if they were enacting a deeper injustice by attempting to address a perceived one?

IN NOVEMBER 2015, I was at work when I received a message from a friend. The friend, like me, was a graduate of the University of British Columbia's Master of Fine Arts in Creative Writing. She told me that Steven Galloway, my former professor and friend, had been suspended from UBC pending an investigation into what the university referred to as "serious allegations." Those allegations, I later learned, included sexual assault. (An investigation by a retired Supreme Court Justice, Mary Ellen Boyd, concluded that the allegations of assault were unsubstantiated.) When my friend told me Galloway had been suspended, I felt dizzy. I hid in the washroom, crying and gathering my thoughts, and then briefly talked to my supervisor and went home for the night. Fuck, I kept thinking. Fuck fuck fuck. I didn't know the woman who'd made the initial accusation very well. I had been much closer to Galloway. I house-sat for him, walked his dog. He'd volunteered—not because I was doing it for class credit, not because he was my thesis advisor—to read my novel-in-progress. I'd gone sailing with him and other students. Drank at the Legion with him on Thursdays. But: I felt dizzy and ill because the first thing that had come to mind, when I learned of the allegations, was the time Galloway slapped my friend across the face at the Legion right after she'd graduated.

I'd buried that moment. I was surprised when it resurfaced. I hadn't wanted to watch it directly; I was sitting across the table, to the right, and instead of turning my head, I let it happen just inside my line of vision. So my memory brought the sound of the slap, and the silence that followed it. I'd known it was coming—he'd indicated it was coming, though I wasn't sure what had passed between them that led to that point. I thought it was going to be a pantomime, something gentle, a joke; instead, it felt like it carried the force of real animosity. The silence after the slap lasted too long, and then my friend laughed it off. She has a boisterous, energetic cackle, the kind that focuses the energy of a room. She laughed it off, and we kept drinking. Fuck. Fuck fuck fuck.

In June 2016, Galloway was fired after the investigations into his conduct had concluded; although UBC cited "a record of misconduct that resulted in an irreparable breach of the trust placed in faculty members," the exact reasons for why they let him go (with no severance) were never made public. In the wake of his firing, he received mostly favourable media coverage and was generally depicted as a victim. (Eventually, it turned out that what many of us suspected—that the slap had been the only substantiated allegation, as it had happened in public, in front of many witnesses—wasn't accurate; the only substantiated allegation was that Galloway had had an affair with a student. I remember thinking, How do you unsubstantiate a slap?)

The project of CanLit felt like it underwent a visible implosion. Galloway's supporters developed alternative theories for his suspension on Facebook. Karen Connelly, an author and Galloway supporter, advanced the gender-swapped "idea for a macabre, best-selling novel" in which two "male" professors in a university department, jealous and power-hungry, had stitched up their "female" boss in order to take "her" place as chair of the department. "Forget the novel," wrote Hal Wake, then the artistic director of the Vancouver Writers Festival, "go straight to TV."

In November 2016, dozens of Canadian writers signed an open letter, called UBC Accountable, supporting Galloway and—though the university had conducted a full investigation before he was fired, and Galloway was, at the time, going through a grievance process supported by the faculty union—calling for "due process and fair treatment for all, which the University appears to have denied Professor Galloway." The letter's signatories included such Canadian luminaries as Margaret Atwood, David Cronenberg, Madeleine Thien, John Vaillant, David Bezmozgis, Yann Martel, and even some UBC creative writing profs. At times, it seemed like the entirety of CanLit—and then, as the story gained traction, a good portion of the putrid swamp of online men's rights activists—stood behind Galloway, across a lonely aisle from a handful of complainants who had relatively little power, and were mostly being supported by writers and academics who were far more likely than the letter's signatories to be women, to be non-binary, to be trans, to be of colour, to be queer.

But it wasn't just Galloway and the open letter that tore a rift through the centre of CanLit in that period. There was also the Appropriation Prize debacle of 2017, in which the editor of the Writers' Union of Canada magazine proposed, in an editorial introducing an Indigenous voices issue, that there should be an "Appropriation prize for best book by an author who writes about people who aren't even remotely like her or him." Although the editor received swift criticism—and apologized, and resigned from his position—several of the nation's most prominent editors, including the then editors-in-chief of the Walrus and the National

Post, and the editor-in-chief of Maclean's, publicly signed on to establish the prize.

In 2018, two more professors—Jon Paul Fiorentino and David McGimpsey, who taught at Concordia University in Montreal—were suspended pending sexual misconduct allegations. Toronto independent publisher Coach House Books placed its poetry program on hiatus after one of its poetry board members and editors, Jeramy Dodds, appeared on a list of "shitty media men."

And then came the defamation suits. Dodds filed a $13.5 million suit against the Globe and Mail and the Toronto Star for reporting on allegations against him, and against four unidentified women for making them. Galloway's labour arbitration with UBC resulted in his receipt of $167,000 in damages "for statements the school made during the process that violated his privacy rights and harmed his reputation"; he subsequently filed a defamation suit against the main complainant in his case, as well as twenty-four other people, for "recklessly repeating" the main complainant's accusations—in some cases on Twitter, in some cases in private to others, in one case as part of an art exhibition. On the subject of "due process," it is worth noting that none of the complainants initially received copies of their sections of Mary Ellen Boyd's report, which detailed her findings about their complaints, and that Galloway had to give his consent to the university to release them. It's further worth noting that at the time he filed suit, the main complainant—whose report had been redacted— had not yet received an unredacted copy of her own report, with which she could better defend herself in court.

Somewhere in the midst of this series of controversies and lawsuit filings, as I was working as an editor at the Montreal-based general interest magazine *Maisonneuve*, an advance review copy of Nick Mount's *Arrival: The Story of CanLit* landed on my desk. As I read, I recognized several parallels between what I'd been witnessing in contemporary CanLit and what had occurred in the sixties and seventies, the period covered in *Arrival*—a period when CanLit, also via open letter, convinced itself it was fighting American imperialism in Canadian poetics by celebrating Milton Acorn, seemingly forgetting, or giving not one shit about, what they were communicating to his beleaguered and frankly more talented ex-wife, who was first wronged by Acorn and then later treated as collateral damage. Both the UBC Accountable letter and the push to establish the People's Poetry Prize betrayed the same institutional urge within CanLit to protect the powerful, at the same time as the proponents of the fight believed they were doing the opposite.

I felt naive—I'd studied Canadian literature and its many debacles during my English degree, and I never should have been as optimistic about the trajectory of CanLit as I'd been before 2016. I'd thought it had been getting better in the half a century that had passed since much of what was chronicled in *Arrival*, but what unfolded after Galloway was suspended from his teaching post at UBC made it seem like not much had changed.

THE PARALLELS FELT UNDENIABLE: an open letter that never should have been written, and the elevation of the perspective and feelings of a badly behaving man over the people he'd treated poorly, to the detriment of the people he'd treated poorly.

And white people claiming Indigenous ancestry. Milton Acorn had been convinced that he had "native blood." "[T]he Indian in me is now authenticated ... It makes me (maybe) one-eighth; but as I've told you, an analysis of physical features makes a much higher content probable. I was born with brown eyes! Not a 'blue-eyed baby' but a brown-eyed papoose," he wrote to Al Purdy, who wrote back, "You seem to continually mention your Indian ancestry, Milt, beginning to seem a little like Grey Owl, a full-blooded Englishman who claimed to be Indian. My point being that whatever virtues Indians have—and they have plenty—you must have your own." (Acorn's biographers generally come to the conclusion that this ancestry was part of Acorn's self-mythology; despite what he wrote to Purdy, his family tree doesn't indicate any Indigenous ancestors at all.)

Partway through the unfurling of the Galloway sympathy brigade, it was revealed that Galloway had First Nations ancestry; the novelist who shared this information, though, was Joseph Boyden, and the information was positioned to be used as a protective cudgel against Galloway's complainants, somehow. (One of Galloway's friends wrote at the time, in a tweet that has now been deleted: "it's been edifying watching Canadians condemn us for standing up for the simple rights of an indigenous man.") Joseph Boyden's own claims to Indigenous heritage were subsequently interrogated and found to be specious.

It is telling that CanLit is a colonial project—that it was founded and funded as a means to shore up Canadian culture against incursions from US literature—and that these writers, who previously moved through the world comfortably as white men, appealed to Indigeneity as a shield, or a fantastical way to bolster interest in their biographies and ancestries and work, to fuel creative production. This move isn't new—Confederation Poet Duncan Campbell Scott, an Indian agent who enacted policies that worked towards the genocide of Indigenous Peoples with his left hand, wrote celebrated elegiac poetry about the coming end of the Indigenous way of life in Canada with his right hand.

Moreover, Canada is small: some of the same people who were active in the People's Poet Award celebration were vocal when Galloway was suspended. Margaret Atwood, for one. Atwood, who compared UBC's investigation process to the Salem witch trials, even as, south of the border, the TV adaptation of *The Handmaid's Tale* was winning her a new generation of fans among a certain segment of feminists.

The parallels—less between Acorn and Galloway than between the CanLit response to them—felt clear to me, but then another harassment-in-academia scandal happened, this time at NYU, and the machinery of power lurched into action again, hauntingly similar to the way it had with Galloway. Avital Ronell, a feminist philosopher and star comparative literature professor, was accused of harassment, sexual assault, and stalking by a former master's student. Almost immediately, a litany of famous scholars—including Judith Butler, Gayatri Chakravorty Spivak, and Slavoj Žižek—wrote an open letter defending Ronell. "We have all seen her relationship with students, and some of us know the individual who has waged this malicious campaign against her," they wrote. "We hold that the allegations against her do not constitute actual evidence, but rather support the view that malicious intention has animated and sustained this legal nightmare."

Some of these signatories, who had made their careers analyzing how power worked, couldn't see it from the inside. Like the signatories of the Galloway open letter, they positioned Ronell as the wronged party. "She deserves a fair hearing, one that expresses respect, dignity, and human solicitude in addition to our enduring admiration," wrote Ronell's defenders. But this was a fanciful reformation of the situations that had led to Galloway's and Ronell's suspensions in the first place—they'd both been accused of wielding their power as professors over some of their students in order to harass and assault them. In the case of UBC, as the signatories of Galloway's open letter decried his unfair treatment and talked about the Boyd Report on Twitter, implying that they'd seen it, these same (now-graduated) student complainants hadn't yet received their own sections of the report, and were mostly learning about updates on their complaints via social media and newspapers rather than directly through the university.

More broadly, outside the university, outside the group of people who were directly affected by what had happened at UBC, young and emerging writers were receiving object lessons in what would happen if they tried to address situations in which they'd been abused, harassed, or assaulted by a more established, socially connected, powerful writer. But it's also important to say that it wasn't the late sixties anymore; while Galloway's supporters, by virtue of their advanced careers and social positions, had more access to platforms like the Globe and Mail, less established writers had social media, particularly Twitter.

Some people—the type of liberal who used to say, maybe as recently as a decade ago, that they liked to "give voice to the voiceless" in their writing, and the type of conservative who feels aggrieved when someone younger and smarter dunks on their received wisdom—called the voices who emerged through social media a "mob." When I imagine what it would have been like without a platform for those voices, it becomes clear that these voices, speaking back to power, were not a mob at all; what the folks who called them that are really taking issue with are the few hardscrabble checks that have emerged to interfere with the workings of the levers of power.

IN 2017, I WENT ON A MONTH-LONG RESIDENCY at the Al Purdy A-frame house in Ameliasburgh, Ontario. The A-frame is somewhat legendary; Purdy and his wife, Eurithe, and her father and brothers, built it from scratch, scrounging free and cheap materials, and then they opened their home to generations of Canadian writers. Generally—reflective of the state of CanLit at the time—white male writers.

Today, a group of dedicated volunteers keeps the house alive and the residency thriving. It offers a stipend, travel costs, and four solitary weeks to focus on one's manuscript. When I was at the A-frame, I was visibly queer, visibly pregnant. Even if someone mistook me for a woman, they would never mistake me for the kind of woman that the men of sixties and seventies CanLit would have given a second look. Yet there I was, filling the house with queer pregnant energy, writing and editing poems, reading another, unpublished book—the notebook documenting previous poets-in-residence's recommendations and experiences. I wasn't the only pregnant writer to do a residency at the A-frame, and when another poet came with their young kid, the volunteers bought a toddler bed. The list of poets-in-residence was full of women, of introspective men, several of them queer. The list provided a very different energy from what I'd gleaned it was like in Al Purdy's time.

The A-frame felt chockablock full of the energy from all the writers who'd been there previously. More familiar with their poetry than their escapades, I read a copy of The Al Purdy A-Frame Anthology and pictured Purdy arguing with his male poet guests around the kitchen table, surrounded by empties—beer and the wine Purdy made himself with foraged wild grapes—while Eurithe, who didn't really drink, sought peace in the kitchen or bedroom.

Most of the contributors to the anthology are men. George Bowering has a short piece about visiting with his then-partner, Angela. "When Angela in her short skirt climbed to look at the loft we would sleep in eventually, Al the perfect host held the ladder and watched to make sure that she didn't slip," writes Bowering. "When she went to use the outhouse, he manfully flung the door open so I could get a picture for, uh, posterity." It was 1967, two years before the entirety of CanLit, including Purdy, decided that Acorn was more deserving of a Governor General's Award than Bowering, or McEwen.

I thought a lot about Margaret Atwood, a friend of Purdy's, a contributor to the A-Frame Anthology, a connective thread between both the People's Poet and Galloway open letter incidents. I'd concluded that she believed herself to be exceptional—both in terms of talent and gender position. She'd navigated the sexism of CanLit, managing to more than hold her own; perhaps she felt that her contemporaries, and everyone who came after, should have figured out how to do the same. Atwood also seemed to reproduce in her writing, at the same frequency as her white male peers, many of the tropes of CanLit as colonial project.

I was thinking about all this when I read the letters in Yours, Al, that Purdy exchanged with Atwood, Acorn, and Earle Birney. And when I read The Red Shoes, Rosemary Sullivan's biography of Atwood's early years. In Atwood's letters to Purdy and to Layton, her prose strikes an assertive and funny note, with insights that probably flattered their recipients at the same time as they set the tone—Atwood was in charge—for their relationships. Purdy and Layton's letters feel infinitely more tossed-off, written from a place of assumed rather than earned confidence. Atwood studiously avoided dating any of these men. Purdy wrote a mean-spirited and generally unfunny poem about her, called "Concerning Ms. Atwood," that basically decries her as a self-involved, egotistical social climber— one who meets God and then must write God's name down in "her little notebook" so as to not forget it. (Again, it feels like not much, vis-à-vis the misogyny reserved for self-confident women writers, has changed: the tone of this poem reminded me of Zachariah Wells's "Citric Bitch's Thinking Is Shit," written in 2009 about poet and critic Sina Queyras, which ends with an exhortation to kiss the author's dick.)

In Rosemary Sullivan's biography of Atwood, Acorn comes up a handful of times, nearly always in reference to MacEwen's relationship with him. In contrast, the book details a close friendship between the two women, one where they discussed everything from myth and creativity to their work to the men around them. In a letter included in Yours, Al, Atwood champions MacEwen's writing to Purdy; she wrote essays about it; later, she edited a collection of MacEwen's poetry. Why, then, did she fete Acorn at a celebration designed to assuage his ego because he'd lost an award to his younger, more talented ex-wife?

When Atwood likened UBC's treatment of Galloway to a witch hunt, it was ironic to the complainants and observers, who were used to seeing complainants—and perhaps women, more broadly—portrayed as witches. More ironic still is the fact that one of Atwood's most famous poems— "Half-hanged Mary"—is based on her ancestor Mary Reeve Webster, who according to Rosemary Sullivan, was "tried as a witch a decade before the infamous Salem witch trials of 1692–93." Did half-hanged Mary flit into

Atwood's mind as she invoked the witch trials to position Galloway as the victim of a bunch of mostly women he'd in fact had the power over? Phrased another way: Why bother invoking witches at all when CanLit's own history has so many similar situations that could have been invoked either directly or by metaphor?

On the one hand, Atwood thrived in CanLit at a time when the men around her were addressing her in letters with lines like, "I think you're a beautiful woman ... You weren't always, I don't think, but you've become one over the years. Why shouldn't older male writers dream of getting you into bed, and younger ones want to show you their poems?" On the other, she's been complicit in reproducing the sexism, racism, and colonialism that has underpinned the project of CanLit, making it stifling, unwelcoming, limited, limiting. This is why, I think, she became a secondary lightning rod as the events of Galloway's suspension and eventual firing unfolded, dishing it out as well as she took it: she represents the compromises a white woman can make in order to succeed in CanLit, and to uphold it so as to preserve her success. That positioning has found no quarter among writers who'd rather dismantle CanLit altogether, and those who have never, perhaps, quite been in the position to employ these kinds of strategies and compromises to achieve success. Phrased as a callback to 1969: If Milton Acorn was the People's Poet, then what was the People's Poetry? Who were the People?

WHAT DO WE OWE THE PEOPLE WHO CAME BEFORE US, and what do they owe us? The complexities of life and care and relationship are what are supposed to inform our work, and perhaps they do—it's been suggested to me that Miriam Toews's Women Talking, a fictionalized account of Mennonite women meeting to discuss how to deal with a systemic series of rapes in their community, is in part a novel-length response of sorts to the fact that she initially signed the Galloway letter. But I also feel itchy about accepting reformations or apologies or feminist analyses through literary texts. If one's initial support for Galloway—or, sorry, "due process"—occurred publicly, and explicitly, then one's modulation of opinion or position should occur publicly and explicitly, too.

But then, it can be difficult to be outspoken, confrontational, in a community as small as CanLit. For example, over a year after I read my former professor Andreas Schroeder's UBC Accountable statement—a statement that asked for "justice" but cited the complainants' allegations as "unconvincing," "trivial," or "irrelevant"—I found myself standing next to him at the main stage of a literary festival. Remembering his class, which resulted in my first successful feature pitch, I was initially pleased to see him—but the silence of saying nothing about his UBCA signature or statement immediately began to gnaw at me.

Regardless of what, exactly, happens with the project of CanLit—a colonial project, a project that reflected the sexism and racism of the era in which it was born, and the following eras in which it was mythologized—the reality is that everyone who has been affected negatively by that letter will be asked to share stages, green rooms, festival space, editors, agents, and publishers with the writers who signed it. Several years out from the initial cacophony of voices in our national papers and on social media, the writers who signed the UBC Accountable letter mostly seem like they'd prefer to never speak about it again. So, in green rooms and festival spaces, on stages and at readings, polite silence falls like fresh snow.

But I do not want to pretend as though the letter—which was actively harmful to both the complainants and to a broader swath of early-career writers and writing students witnessing the ways in which power supports power at the expense of the expendable—does not exist, or is no longer worth talking about. When I ask myself what I owe and who I owe it to, the answer is clear. I owe my colleagues, whose complaints have been dismissed as "unconvincing," "trivial," and "irrelevant," visible and audible support (as well as whatever financial aid I can offer as they are sued). I owe polite silence nothing.

kyle

KYLE WAS BORN IN 1987 IN OAKVILLE, ONTARIO. His dad was a police officer there, but he didn't want to raise kids in the city, so he moved them to a farm in the Fergus-Arthur area. Growing up in Arthur was challenging. Kyle remembers, from an early age, people telling him he was gay, because he was a little feminine as a child. He was also very sensitive. He got teased a lot. His parents, doing what they thought was best for him, pushed him to be involved in heteronormative things like sports. Kyle always knew he was different.

One memory that sticks out to him is being seven, eight, nine years old and being forced to play hockey. He was good at it, but there was pressure: you're a boy, you play hockey. He remembers crying to his parents one night when he was a small kid. He'd always been pretty self-aware in telling his dad that he wanted to do things like ballet, things that were more transgressive. His parents are great now, but at the time they said,

"Boys don't do that. You're not a fag." He remembers getting into an argument with his dad and his dad dropped the word "cocksucker." That was the point Kyle shifted inwards, and realized that he had to do everything he could to get out of Arthur, so that he could be himself.

Arthur is a town of about roughly 2,000 people. It's an intersection, really. His high school had about 200 people. His classes were about ten to twelve students. Everybody was heavily invested in each other's lives. The town was very white and Christian. Kyle's neighbours were Mennonites. The kids didn't go to school past grade eight. Girls swam with their dresses on.

Kyle grew up Catholic. His dad is Catholic, and he baptized his kids so that they could go to the Catholic school, because he thought it would provide a better education. Kyle stopped going to Catholic school after grade nine because he no longer believed in the tenets. Sex education, in his generation, was incredibly lacking and offensive. He remembers his eighth grade teacher telling him that the only reason for any sexual activity was for procreation. He remembers thinking that any act other than vaginal-penile intercourse was wrong, because it wasn't for procreation, and that's what God says.

Kyle wasn't the best student growing up, but as soon as he got to grade nine, he started to focus on academics. Gay-bashing was still tolerated when he was in high school, so in order to get out, Kyle knew he had to excel.

Kyle was seventeen when he moved out of his parents' house. He never went back to live there, after moving to London, Ontario, for university. London was still pretty small, in the grand scheme of things. Ultimately, when he was young, he always knew that he would probably end up in one of three cities: Montreal, Toronto, or Vancouver. Kyle looks at young gay people who are coming out of small towns, and he looks at his circle of friends, and the common thread seems to be that getting to the city provides some sort of anonymity, and some sort of security blanket, and the opportunity to meet other queer people.

Kyle's plan was to focus on school, to the detriment of other things, like socializing. He likes to say that he's thirty now, but because of everything he went through, he's probably mentally only about twenty, in terms of actual development. From the time Kyle was seventeen to the time he was about twenty-four, he battled exclusively with the question of his sexuality in his head. He didn't do well in school. He didn't connect well socially. He hopes that kids today have a period during high school where they can act out and explore themselves. Kyle never had that. He didn't have any queer or gay role models in his life. He wanted to make sure he could support himself financially before coming out. Kyle had heard horror stories. So it took him quite a while. He came out when was twenty-six or twenty-seven. It stunted a lot of his growth. And here he is at thirty-two, feeling like he's just starting his life for the first time.

If you'd asked Kyle a year or two ago if he felt confident walking down the streets of Arthur holding his partner's hand, he would have said yes. But now he can't tell you the last time, since Doug Ford was elected premier of Ontario in 2018, that he's felt comfortable enough, even in Toronto, to hold his partner's hand. People feel emboldened to comment on things or insert themselves into conversations where they have no place. The Fords are populist, and the lowest common denominator is the religious right. He would be scared now to go back to his hometown with his partner.

Kyle thinks that if he were a young person today, and he were gay, and he had the ability to at least explore or question his identity as a ten-, twelve-, thirteen-year-old, then things might have turned out a lot different for him. He had a lot of wasted potential, a lot of wasted years. He hopes the current political climate doesn't stop young people from coming out, from being themselves. He hopes it doesn't scare young people, but it does scare him. It's not just that rolling back sex education can hurt people, it's that it gives people the authority to hurt themselves, or reach out and hurt others.

There were so many years where, instead of hating himself, he could have been hating the conservative government, and really helping move the needle forward. He's met so many people his age, his generation, who fell into substance abuse issues, self-harm, depression. So many of his friends that he's seen going to the bars now, for the last five years, roughly, since he's been out, do the same thing, just over and over and over again, like it's Groundhog Day. Some of them are trying to grow up, even in their thirties. But it requires making a very conscious decision that you're going to grow up, because the process of growing up in the eighties and nineties was not "normal" for queer youth, and it's therefore easier to get stuck in a kind of permanent adolescence. Many of his friends have been making the shift towards trying to build a healthier life, but many of them have also not been able to dig themselves out of the hole. As for Kyle himself, to this day he knows he can't take a drink without wanting to drink the entire bottle. Although he doesn't abuse liquor now, if he does drink it, he has to be very cautious about his intake.

Kyle's dad was a police officer and his mom was a dispatcher. That's how they met in Toronto. And then they continued similar jobs out in the country. Kyle believes strongly in the power of public service. Becoming a law enforcement officer was the route he wanted to go. And as he was moving towards self-acceptance, he wanted to be a role model for that kid in grade eight, who's watching the Pride parade and sees a cop marching in it.

For Kyle, becoming a police officer was also a matter of breaking barriers. He faced very strong resistance within the Toronto police. Not necessarily always explicit, which there was, but even the implicit things, where people would be invited out after work for a beer, and suddenly the gay guys weren't invited. He wanted to challenge heteronormative stereotypes, in a very straight environment, or at least, an environment that wasn't very open to gay men. He used his time at the Toronto police to be a disrupter, to engage in positive social change. He walked in the parade for a few years with his partner. He went down to New York City and represented Toronto in the Pride parade there. He used that opportunity, that uniform he was given, to make a statement. It was definitely challenging in that environment, but Kyle's glad he was able to work on anti-bullying while he was part of the force, as well as walk in the parade.

rhean

RHEAN IS BIGENDER. Like a lot of queer people, they spent many early years feeling confused, and not having any language to talk about it. And then all of a sudden, they found Twitter, and were like, "Oh. Look at these people. Just having these conversations. Well, this is great." And then at least they have some language, such that when it comes up with their mother, they don't have a screaming match where she's like, "Do you just want to be a boy?" and rhean responds, "Ugh, God, why? Why?"

rhean is Two-Spirit, but that's complicated. They were born in 1980, in Penticton, but they only met their birth mother five years ago. When rhean was born, their biological mother couldn't take care of them, so she gave them up for adoption, to what her employers told her was a wealthy family. Initially, the family could have been described as wealthy, but then their alcoholism and personality issues drove them apart. rhean's adoptive parents weren't even together for a full year after they adopted rhean. And then the woman rhean called their mother—rhean no longer thinks of her as their mother—moved to Vancouver. Their childhood was split in two, between a cosmopolitan, coastal city, and Summerland, BC, where there were fifteen churches in a town of less than 30,000.

rhean has had people contact them on Twitter and be like, "What tribe are you from?" And they explain their history and how they were disconnected from their culture. rhean doesn't want to be one of those horning-in, johnny-come-lately Native people. There's a *Seinfeld* episode where a guy converts to Judaism so that he can tell Jewish jokes. rhean doesn't want to be that person.

As a performance artist, rhean connects with the idea that gender can be performative. You can be very neutral, and just be yourself, come as you are, and then you can do all of the signifiers that make you more of what is acceptable, or you can play around with it and be something that nobody's ever seen from a Joan D. Vinge sci-fi novel. rhean wants to get to that world, with the silver skin and the sail fins.

After rhean's parents split up, their adoptive mother moved to a rural area of Metro Vancouver. rhean went to school there until they were fourteen. They spent so much time in the office at elementary school that the secretaries had them start answering the phone. Eventually, one of rhean's teachers designated them a gifted learner, and they were sent to the Richmond district learning program. It was the first time in their life that they felt like they were in a room full of people who were just like them.

And then rhean's adoptive mother died by suicide. rhean's adoptive father brought them back to the Okanagan, but he was neglectful. He lived in a shack and wouldn't give up his bedroom. Instead, he put a trailer on the side of the house. He kept his beer and smokes outside of the house in a beer fridge and a freezer. rhean would wait for the sun to go down, when the lights would be on and their adoptive father couldn't see out, and rhean would take whatever they wanted. The teachers at rhean's school were upset. "I can see your potential, and you're just wasting yourself." Finally, rhean was like, "Yeah, Summerland is not where I want to die, so I need to smarten up."

rhean got in touch with a woman who used to take care of them when they were younger, and they emancipated themselves and became her foster kid. And then rhean was an honour student, and they graduated and got the hell out of there.

rhean calls the woman who took care of them before and after they were emancipated Mom. rhean and their mom are both very stubborn, so sometimes they'll go for a few years without speaking to each other, because one or the other will have done something that in hindsight is actually really small and not anything to stop speaking to somebody over. rhean calls her Mom because she put in the most care as a mother. They had discussions about gender in high school. rhean's mom wanted them to present ultra-feminine, like she did. To get up in the morning, put on makeup, put on a skirt. The first thing rhean did when they moved out was cut their hair, which was so long they could sit on it. They got an orange mohawk and decided to never wear makeup again, unless they were playing a woman part.

As long as rhean presents as a mostly heteronormative cis person, it keeps their mom happy. Drag is a persona that they can accept; rhean doesn't live as a man, and they don't have dysphoria with their body, and they don't talk about being bigender with their mom.

rhean does, though, feel a bit jealous of young trans people. They feel like a fangirl. They're like, "You guys are so brave. I'll just be over here in the corner." It's hard, even, to have conversations about it. To have the vocabulary to talk about it. There's a colour analogy. Blue didn't exist until around 6,000 years ago. People just didn't see blue. There are studies that show that certain people who don't have enough vocabulary for green only see two or three shades of green. And then, if you give them the words for it, all of a sudden, they're actually able to perceive more.

After rhean graduated from high school, they immediately moved to Calgary. They attended the Alberta College of Art + Design. It was a really broad program, and rhean wanted to work with their hands. rhean still lives in Calgary. If you want to paint horses and landscapes, maybe some flowers, you might be successful. If you paint horses, you can pay for your entire year of living just by doing the Western showcase at the Stampede. But then you'll be pigeonholed into painting horses your entire life.

Calgary feels to rhean like the biggest small town in Canada, but it's also okay. Prairie people mind their own business more. And maybe that becomes a problem, minding your own business, if someone's being harassed.

rhean is now at a point in their life where they can have a couple drinks. For children of alcoholics, it's complicated. In high school, when they decided they needed to get out of town, they quit drinking, period. They wouldn't use mouthwash or eat desserts or anything cooked with alcohol. Then as they got older, they were like, "Well, this is just another form of extremism." They allowed themselves to relax a bit. And then they got dumped in a letter. It was horrendous. They didn't eat solid food for twenty-eight days, and they drank a lot of alcohol during that time. They worked on a ski hill and had fun drinking. They had a little window—it wasn't like a big, bay window; it was just like a side window—into their adoptive parents' life, where they were like, "When you have issues, there's this warm fuzzy blanket called being drunk, and it feels fun." But then you sober up, and the issues are still there, so then you get drunk again.

rhean's adoptive dad used to tell funny stories about his father and the strap that used to hang by the back door, and rhean would be like, "That's abuse." Their father would be like, "That's discipline." rhean's adoptive mother took antidepressants and drank alcohol heavily, and it destroyed her brain. She was highly intelligent as a child, but at the end she couldn't do basic math anymore. rhean thinks that contributed to her suicide. rhean has complicated feelings about suicide. It's someone's life and they can do what they want with it. If you don't want to be here, why are we telling you to stay? For rhean, they always wonder what's around the next corner. Maybe there's something around the next corner. What's around that next corner?

rhean read something on Twitter about the Jewish approach to forgiveness. The person who needs to be forgiven has to do the work of making amends and come to the person they hurt and be like, "Will you forgive me?" If they ask three times and you turn them away, then it's on your head, because they've done the work. But if there's no work done, you don't let it go like, "Oh, you know, that's how people are."

rhean's problem is that the people they need to forgive are dead. rhean doesn't feel like their adoption was a nefarious experiment. Their adoptive parents weren't like, "We're going to adopt this baby, and then we're going to ruin its life." After rhean's adoptive dad died a slow death from alcoholism, rhean got some books from him, and there's a book of poetry and some art prints. rhean's dad never expressed any interest in art and made fun of rhean for being artistic. Never expressed any interest in poetry and made fun of them for being interested in it. rhean holds those things and wonders, *What ruined you as a human being, and why did you listen to those other people?*

rhean's biological family likes to get together, so every two years they're like, "No, you can't get out of it, you have to come and spend ten days with us." Last year it was snowboarding. They're really chill. They're like rhean, if rhean hadn't been abused. And they appreciate rhean's dark sense of humour. But rhean doesn't have the warm fuzzies about it exactly. It's really nice, but they're a bunch of adults that rhean met as an adult. There is one adult from rhean's childhood who stands out as having shown rhean an example of what they could be. Cheryl, who lived in the suite above rhean's adoptive grandmother in Vancouver. It wasn't until later that rhean realized Cheryl was a lesbian. Cheryl was rhean's positive female role model. Cheryl was the one who first gave rhean a window into other ways of being. Living in a totally insular community without access, without positive representation in books and movies and conversations, you end up not being able to express yourself properly. Cheryl seemed so much happier, not pretending.

13

37 JOBS AND 21 HOUSES

THE HOUSE I GREW UP IN was built in the early eighties. It was at the edge of a brand new suburb in Dundas, Ontario, and was meant to be a starter house (I don't think we think of houses in that way anymore—they're less stepping stones than an end goal that may or may not be attainable at all). The house had a porch at the front and a deck at the back, and the garage was painted grey-blue. There was a small bathroom, kitchen, and living/dining room on the first floor, and then three small bedrooms and a full-sized bathroom upstairs. The basement was partially finished; we spent a lot of time there because that's where the TV was. My earliest memory is from when I was a toddler and sat on a bee in the backyard, on the grass. My parents must have felt an overpowering optimism, buying the house. They must have been thinking of the family they would have, the home they would build together.

I spent the first seventeen years of my life living in that house. We were always almost losing it. We couldn't pay the mortgage or the bills. Collection agencies called the landline and I answered after school, before my parents got home. Bills came and my mother told me to hide them under the recycling bin on a shelf in the garage. The house became tense. The house was a proxy for our relationships with another, the ways in which our family wasn't functioning.

The other problem with the house was that it was in a small town. In a small town, everybody knows your business. In a small town, which is made of even smaller, interconnected communities, you are the product of your parents and other familial connections. As a kid, you understand instinctively that if your parents are marked, you are marked, too. I felt marked; throughout high school, my mother was having an affair with my best friend's father and I thought that if I knew, everyone else must know, too. My mother and my best friend's father drank at the Air Force Club, in the basement, down a flight of stairs. The Air Force Club was close to my best friend's father's produce store, where she and I and our brothers both worked. While we were working, they were drinking.

The day after my mother's affair with my best friend's father finally came to light—definitive and undeniable, rather than an open secret—my dad drove down to the produce store. My dad walked in and my best friend's uncle, who was running the till, greeted my father warmly, pointed in the direction of the Air Force Club, and said, "He's over there." But my dad wasn't there to haul my future stepfather out of the bar by the collar. My dad was there to set the tone for how life post-affair would unfurl for him: he wasn't about to hide his face from the places he was used to going, up to and including his wife's boyfriend's store, where both of his kids had worked alongside their best friends. His life would continue on as it had, and he would carry no shame for a situation he wasn't responsible for.

This is really the only way to survive living in a small town. But the other way to survive is to not live in a small town at all, to move away.

When you are poor or broke—two conditions that are similar but not the same—one of the only ways to get free of the situation you feel stuck in is to work, if you can, and then work some more. I cannot write about moving without writing about working, because I had to work in order to move at all.

I WORKED MY FIRST FIVE JOBS BEFORE I LEFT HOME. I was hired to do janitorial work at a small orthotics and custom shoe manufacturer a few days a week after school. My co-workers included a hippie who lived on a type of co-op land share and who lent me books, an extroverted Persian man who taught me how to write my name in Farsi (I forget now), and a quiet, fastidious woman who kept everyone in check if they forgot that I both was and wasn't their peer. I would have stayed there as long as I lived in Dundas, but I made the mistake of babysitting for the owner and his wife; his wife lost her temper one day when she came home and the playroom of their pristine home was messy, and I quit the job because I didn't know how to tell the owner I never wanted to be yelled at by his terrifying wife ever again, because I got enough of that at home.

My second job was at Tim Hortons: more yelling. The owners were a husband and wife; the husband did spot checks to make sure we kept the bathrooms locked, and then yelled at his sixteen-year-old workers about "crack whores" and needles when we didn't. Once, I cried after the wife yelled at me; my supervisor told me not to let her catch me crying, or things would get worse. (I try to picture, now, being in my forties or fifties and screaming at teens; I can't picture it.)

I started my third job while I was at Tim Hortons. I'd wanted to work at my best friend's father's store, to be closer to my friend. I'm not sure if my mother started having an affair with her dad before or after I started working at the store. The meaning of working at the store changed after I found out, though. Nobody yelled at me, but when it was my turn to retrieve my mother from the Air Force Club I'd brace myself to see her hand on his forearm, or his on the small of her back. I'd think about the anti–drunk driving demonstrations at school and how they targeted the students, leaving out any mention of how you were supposed to handle it when it was your parent who was too drunk to drive.

My fourth and best job was at Jumbo Video, where I earned minimum wage while eating popcorn and learning about people's movie-watching preferences. My fifth and final job before my first move was at a YMCA summer camp in Burlington. The summer camp had been built around the park's creek, but then the creek became contaminated with runoff from area farms, and we couldn't let the kids in anymore. I was vegan that summer and dyed my hair a purple that soon turned grey. My favourite activity was fort-building because it kept us out of the sun. Midway through the summer, the camp director tricked me into going on a date with him ("They're filming a movie with Sarah Jessica Parker's husband after-hours at camp! Me and a bunch of us are going to watch them film for a bit!"), and then kissed me as I dissociated. He said, "I'll have to get someone else to do your job review now."

When I left Dundas, I thought I would get farther than Guelph, but Guelph was as far as I got. My hair was still purple-grey when I arrived, but

I left everything else behind. I left my old self behind. Everyone in Dundas knew how embarrassing I was, how weird I'd been as a kid, how fucked-up my family was. There were people at a local restaurant who thought that my best friend, not me, was my mother's daughter, and my mother let them think she was. When I left I went bankrupt on my social debts. The camp director found me in the university directory and left a message on my dorm room phone: "andrea!" he said. "I'm coming to town to visit!" I deleted that message, and the next one.

IN GUELPH I LIVED IN A RESIDENCE CALLED ARTZ HAÜS, with other writers, artists, and theatre kids. I didn't have to work until partway through the semester, when I needed an emergency root canal and immediately exhausted my savings. In the time that I was not working, I was learning how to be a university student. I dated a slightly older first-year student. I wandered through the arboretum at the eastern edge of campus and slept under the stars. Barely anyone I'd met in Artz Haüs had a job. I met other kids, from other residences, who'd come from working-class families. We clustered together as if for warmth. We got stoned outside. My groups of friends did not exactly understand one another, and I was not a good bridge between them. At the very end of the year, I went to New York with two friends; one of them opened his wallet and shared the money his father had given him for the trip, and I wanted to cry.

After the trip, I went back home for the summer and worked at Hamilton Parks & Rec, and I returned to Jumbo Video, and I think I even helped out again at my best friend's dad's store. My parents were separated, and it felt like my mother couldn't decide whether to wage a campaign to win her kids' favour or to simply demand our allegiance.

My mother promised my brother a dog if he went to live with her. She complained endlessly about my father. She wanted me to stay over at her house. I stayed over and she got progressively more drunk and angry.

Eventually, the early working hours combined with the late working hours combined with the stress of my relationship with my mother broke me. I didn't understand what was happening, but I became hypomanic. My body said, *You don't want to sleep? Okay.* I had been taking Paxil and two different kinds of anxiety medications. When I finally ended up at the hospital after overdosing accidentally, I was discharged a few hours later to worried family members, including my mother. When I saw her in the hall, I froze. She had her sweet voice on. The next morning I woke up with no hangover because I'd had an IV drip, which was disquieting. I quit the Paxil and the benzodiazepines immediately; I worked less, but I kept working.

THE FIRST HOUSE WE LIVED IN—two friends, two friends of friends, and me—after living in university residence had a hole in the wall. We hadn't noticed the hole, which was large, when we viewed the house, because the students who'd lived there had a bunch of junk piled in front of it. My friend and I adopted a cat, and the cat caught a lot of mice. The hole went nowhere, or anywhere—how were we to know? We called our landlord. We emailed our landlord. I joined an anti-poverty and tenants' rights group, and we drew up a formal letter to our landlord and walked to his house and knocked on the door. "What right," his wife said when she answered, holding a baby, "what right do you have to come to our *home*?" Audacity got the hole fixed: a fresh new sheet of drywall. Something I learned from renting from landlords, and helping other people write letters to their landlord, is that a lot of landlords don't know the law, or hope that you don't.

After the hole-in-the-wall house, I lived with some of the same people and the same cat in the same neighbourhood but in a much better house. The oldest and most well-put-together person in the house inaugurated a tradition of making elaborate birthday cakes for everyone's birthdays, and that year mine was in the shape of a veggie burger because we lived across from a Harvey's and I ate so many of them. My friends sourced candy from the Bulk Barn; orange licorice allsorts were transformed into a sheet of processed cheese. I should have stayed there, but I left to live with my drinking-too-much boyfriend in a shithole in the east end with cheap rent.

For my second summer I stayed in Guelph and had a regular part-time job at a restaurant called Curry in a Hurry, which I'd started during the school year. But I was broke and needed more work. I bought an old brown Raleigh city cruiser and rode it from the eastern outskirts of the city to the western outskirts, to Value Village, where my friend David worked in the back. I couldn't afford to ride the bus out to Value Village, so I rode my brown Raleigh through neighbourhood streets that ended in cul-de-sacs and looped around to begin more or less where they'd started. At Value Village, I placed the clothes on the racks by size and colour. My manager timed how long it took me to roll a rack and it was barely satisfactory; I could do better. A secret shopper later also timed how long it took me to roll a rack. When we debriefed, I again learned I could do better.

I quit Value Village to make date squares at an organic bakery in the Jesuit Centre at the north end of town. To get to the bakery I walked up through the Catholic cemetery south of the centre. The atmosphere of the entire place was calm and quiet. I made trays and trays—hundreds and hundreds—of date squares. My lanky, musically talented friend Karl worked there; I also remember the woman who made the pies, who was the only person at the bakery who was occasionally loud and combative, but also the only person who was good at making pies. I was the only chubby person who worked at the bakery. The Jesuit Centre was located west of Highway 6 and north of a suburban strip mall where the Walmart went, even though a dedicated group of activists had blocked its arrival for many years.

That same summer I also worked at the Subway close to our house. Our house had five legal bedrooms, one illegal bedroom, and eight people living in it. It was in an industrial area of the city, out by both the old penitentiary and the slaughterhouse. The only non-student who lived with us briefly worked at the slaughterhouse. Its employees came into the Subway at the ends of their shifts, or after their shifts had ended and then the bar across the street had closed. One time I was working alone and a man, slurring his words and peacocking in front of his friends, yelled at me to make his sub hotter, I wasn't making it hot enough. I thought, Be careful what you wish for, and engaged in malicious compliance. Another time, a drunk man tried to climb over the counter, but it wasn't yet late enough that I was working alone. Me and the supervisor, who was as thin and blonde as a stalk of wheat, instinctively backed against the wall and yelled until a group of men pulled him back. Another time, I went to close and the key to lock up was not where it should have been and when I called the store's owner he was in Kitchener at a club and unable or unwilling to come and close the store. He told me to figure it out. I thought about turning out the lights and walking out, leaving the front door unlocked.

The blonde-as-a-stalk-of-wheat supervisor had to work early the next morning, but she drove over and locked up and we kept that man's family's investment safer than he deserved.

I was so poor at the beginning of that summer that my breakfasts consisted of two tablespoons of peanut butter the eight-person house had purchased communally from a discount supermarket. My regular staff meal at the Subway was half a veggie sub on an oat and honey bun. The supervisor told me how many calories were in the cookies in a disapproving way, but I ate them for the dopamine. Be thin for whom? The peanut butter only staved off so much hunger. At home, for dinner, we ate heaps of pasta, and I was not the only chubby roommate. One of my chubby roommates ate heaps of perogies and worked in retail, but then she joined Primerica and decided to lose weight.

BEFORE I LEFT GUELPH, I lived in several more apartments and had several more jobs. The last positions I worked were simultaneously as a vegetarian cook on evenings and weekends, and in communications at a not-for-profit that had generous benefits and employer-matched retirement savings plan contributions. The first time my shoes wore out while I was working that job, and I realized that I could just buy another pair, just like that, without indebting myself or skipping meals, I felt wealthy and free. In my job, I used the skills I'd learned making zines to make booklets and posters and bookmarks. I checked texts that had been translated into French and copy edited English. When I worked as a vegetarian cook, I learned that I'd accidentally become good at making soups, and I taught new staff members how to make good soup. I was sick at the time and couldn't digest much, and the job was a way to put the energy I had for cooking for myself somewhere else.

The second reason for my second job was that I was saving up to leave. I'd been in Guelph for seven years, and it felt like my memories were ossifying there, that I'd need to leave if I wanted to lead a creative life. My long-term partner had been a musician and a chess player and an alcoholic, another alcoholic. And then I'd dated someone who turned out to be banal and middle class but even more draining emotionally. I needed to leave the self I'd built in Guelph; I needed to see if I could find a better one somewhere else.

Two years after I graduated, I left for the West Coast, to start school in Vancouver. I re-homed my two rabbits, crying as I watched them head down the street in a minivan, the new pets of a young woman who lived at home with her mom. Hoping that they'd be happy. Hoping that I'd be happy.

In Vancouver I lived first in a room in a house with a woman and her teenage daughter. The following year, I moved in with people I'd met at the bike shop where I'd started volunteering. We called that house the Chandelierium; it was a Vancouver Special, the boxy, aesthetically unpopular multi-family architectural style common to the West Coast. Located off Main Street, it had ornate, wonderfully tacky sconces and chandeliers. My first job in the city was making popcorn and selling tickets at the Ridge Theatre. The Ridge was one of the last reel-to-reel theatres in Canada. The projection room sounded like movie theatres were supposed to sound. There was a crying room, which seemed like an indulgent nod to feelings until I realized it had been designed for people who came to the movies with an infant. I smoked cigarettes on the fire escape with my co-workers.

We could feel it coming—the theatre was too nice to remain as it was; it would soon be torn down for condos. I left the Ridge after a few months when I got hired to do some communications work at UBC for twice as much money—the union had ensured that the wages for student jobs were tied to those of regular workers, guarding their own but also lifting the tide while they were at it. I worked as a teaching assistant, I worked as a poetry editor, I worked as a bike mechanic. I reached the age my mother had been when she had me; I was living with several roommates and writing a poetry book about gender, and friendships, and fractured familial relationships.

A FEW MONTHS BEFORE I GRADUATED FROM UBC, after the cushy union wages–tied jobs dried up, I was hired as an editor at Adbusters. Tim Hortons was the worst job I'd ever had, and Adbusters was the second-worst. One of my first tasks was to read through a book the magazine was producing and offer feedback; I came across a picture of a desert with one line floating mid-air, something like, "It takes a thousand years to produce one inch of soil." When I flagged it for fact-checking, a senior editor told me not to bother: the page had appeared in the magazine before, the same concern had been raised, and the publisher didn't care if it was true. The greater truth was that it sounded good. And that it felt true. The best thing about Adbusters was the other writers and artists who worked there. The second-best thing was that it was close to Granville Island, ironically in a townhouse surrounded by other tony townhouses in a picturesque area of Vancouver where few of the staff could afford to—or would want to—live. When it was warm and sunny we'd wander along the sea wall and get sake ice cream with raisins at the sake place on the island.

After I left Adbusters I qualified for financial support via employment insurance because I was depressed and left in part because the job had triggered, and was exacerbating, my depression. The publisher initially denied my request for a record of employment, so in my application for EI, along with a doctor's note, I included an explanation of why I couldn't provide an ROE and also why that ROE, if provided, would be inaccurate: though I'd had fixed hours and duties, I'd been misclassified as a contractor until I'd "earned" my way into being properly classed as an employee.

I wasn't the only misclassified employee at Adbusters; my colleague tried to apply for EI around the same time as me and was only reclassified after the government untangled the mess many months later, after he already had another job. As I was lying on the floor feeling sorry for myself, I spent part of that time thinking about how I'd written so many lyrical words in service of the magazine publisher's revolution, while the reality of our working conditions was that we had to fight to receive the basic benefits that had been afforded to me at Tim Hortons, or Subway, or any of the other sweaty, highly corporate minimum-wage jobs I ever worked.

I moved in with Will—my partner, now spouse—thinking I'd take three months to recuperate. But I worried too much about what I'd do next, so instead of recuperating, I applied for jobs. I kept track: I applied for 200 jobs. I was surviving on oatmeal, and my rule was that I had to hit my daily quota of applications before I was allowed to eat lunch. Some days it got to be three o'clock and instead of eating lunch, I was lying on my stomach on the floor, crying and hoping Will wouldn't come home early and find me there. (My writing was nominated for a National Magazine Award that year. I tried not to be, but I was convinced that if I won, my life would change. I couldn't afford to go to the ceremony in Toronto, so I followed along online from Will's couch. I didn't win. It would have been nice, but it wouldn't have changed anything.)

Three weeks into my time on EI, I signed on with a temp agency and got sent to an in-person interview at a two-storey building near Olympic Village, a semi-industrial area that the city had begun to re-zone for tony new condos. A nondescript door led to a set of stairs; when I knocked on the correct door at the top of the stairs, a woman in fitted athleisure answered. We shook hands; she had the frenetic energy of a small bird. She walked me through her warehouse and explained the job. I'd be her personal assistant; I'd manage her calendar, keep her on track. She manufactured and imported uniforms for local chains and companies. I had little retail experience, but I had plenty of experience managing bosses. The woman interrupted herself to apologize for never finishing a sentence.

The temp agency recruiter had told me that the job might entail reminding my boss to eat lunch. The woman asked me again in person— would I be comfortable with that? Despite my recent spate of penniless-ness and punishment-by-oatmeal, I had learned the art of keeping myself fed. I would never not feed myself to the best of my abilities. *I can feed this woman*, I thought. *I'll get this woman fed.* In the end, though, I didn't. The recruiter called and told me that I was overqualified, and the woman worried that the job was beneath me, that she'd get used to having me around, and then I'd abandon her.

In the end, mercifully, I was hired at as a communications assistant at a private Jewish secondary school, where the pace of the year was set in part by the curriculum and in part by the Hebrew calendar. And where my boss and her boss both said, we know you're overqualified for this, but we will be happy to have you as long as you are happy to stay. The job was part time, but even part-time staff got benefits. I went to the dentist and it felt better even than abandoning oatmeal.

After I got that job Will and I moved across the street from his bachelor apartment to a two-bedroom where, not even a year later, the roof caught on fire as the building next door burned to the ground. We moved to an apartment in a three-storey mid-century stucco dingbat, in West Coast parlance. We'd moved across the street using dollies. When we moved across the city, we used bikes and a truck. And although I liked working at the Jewish school, and I liked my boss, I deeply missed working on bikes. So I returned to the Bike Kitchen as a mechanic, and to the AMS Bike Co-op as their communications coordinator.

IN MY LATE TWENTIES, I finally began to work the kinds of jobs I'd thought of as dream jobs. I hadn't realized I'd been working towards anything in particular. My desires had always felt like a fire hose I couldn't control—intense but unpredictable because I didn't know how to focus on anything but financial survival and escape. I moved from Vancouver to Montreal, where I worked as an editor at another magazine, one I loved, but like most worthwhile Canadian magazines, it had no money, so I also worked again as a bike mechanic and, seasonally, in a big box bookstore at the mall. By that time, I was a National Magazine Award–winning overflow stock artist. It's common, if you don't have family money or a spouse with a nice job, to work as a server or a bartender or a dishwasher as your freelance pieces win awards and appear in the Globe and Mail.

At thirty-two, freelancing and working my dream magazine job, I got pregnant. The baby arrived, and when she was five months old, I got a new editing job, covering a maternity leave at a book publisher, back across the country. I thought about my grandparents: every single one of them had been born in another country and came to Canada to try to make a better life. My mother had lived her whole life within a 100-kilometre radius of where she'd been born; my father, once he came to Canada, had too. I'd treated the country like one giant game of hopscotch.

Eight months into my new job, Will and I bought a small, blue, eighty-four-year-old house, on a quarter-acre lot in a little town within a day's commute of the city. In what felt like a miracle, I got to stay on at my editing job—working remotely from home and travelling into the city every month or two. The math of how we bought the house is the math of anxiety: I worked frenetically while pregnant, scared of what might happen afterwards, a squirrel hoarding acorns against the apocalypse. While working in Vancouver, we lived in Surrey, with Will's mom. Although we hadn't factored in receiving any help, we did: shelter from Will's mom, furniture from Will's grandparents, a house contingency fund from Will's dad, as every penny of what we had went to the down payment and closing costs. My father had been T-boned two years earlier by a drunk driver in a rural part of Hamilton and, after months of legal wrangling, received a small settlement; he gave us part of it and we bought a new bed, a deer fence, the lumber and plastic sheeting for a ten-by-twelve greenhouse. (Sometimes, in bed at night, I think about the man who hit my father, who developed a bad concussion and PTSD after the accident. I hope he stopped drinking. I hope what he did to my father motivated him to reset his life.)

That spring and summer and fall, as we dug garden beds at the new house, I thought often of my grandfather's organic garden full of carrots and asparagus and tomatoes and zucchini. More than buying the house, even, digging the garden felt like a gesture towards permanence—or, at least, not moving next year, or the year after that. How had my grandparents all known when to stop moving? Was it time to stop moving? I counted the number of jobs I'd held; I counted the number of houses I'd lived in. Thirty-seven jobs, twenty-one houses. Houses with holes and mould, houses that belonged to other people, houses with roommates. Houses where my rent was less than my student loan payment; houses where the poorest roommates lived in illegal bedrooms. The kind of grind that begins to leave your entire body weary in your early twenties, when your labour is what is paying your rent, and what is winning your scholarships, and what is supposed to get you to the type of life that maybe materialized for your grandparents but maybe not, the type of life that may evade you. Had I arrived? Could I stop? What would be enough?

In retrospect—finishing this essay almost a year later, in the winter of 2019, as the bears who live around us are in their dens, their metabolisms slowed; as the deciduous trees are dormant; and as I am slowed down and contemplative, too—I think that I broke part of myself when I oriented my life towards escape, towards finding safety through working so very hard, so that when I finally arrived there, the feeling was so foreign that I wasn't sure what to do with it. I thought the key to a better life was to work and to keep moving—and now that the better life has arrived, I am uncertain how to stop the momentum, what to do with the anxiety that has propelled me here.

In addition to thinking about my grandparents, I think about my parents, and the starter house we couldn't keep. I think about a tweet I read a while ago that said full-time jobs in journalism these days are positioned as an award you receive when you've put in enough work, succeeded enough as a freelancer. I think about how hard it is to be able to afford to go the dentist, how I haven't been in years, how I didn't go as a child. How I'm lucky, how banal this story of work and moving and houses is for people in my generation, how when it ends like this, in permanence and security, you're supposed to feel happiness and gratitude, and I do. I do.

NOTES

1

TOMBOY

1   As Jack Halberstam writes: Jack Halberstam, *Female Masculinity* (Durham, NC: Duke University Press, 1998).

2   Lizzie Garrett Mettler's introduction: Lizzie Garrett Mettler, *Tomboy Style: Beyond the Boundaries of Fashion* (New York: Rizzoli, 2012).

3   Pippi Longstocking: I remember watching *Pippi Longstocking*, which was a twenty-six-episode animated cartoon that ran on YTV in Canada in the late nineties. It was based on the series of books written in Swedish by Astrid Lindgren in the 1940s.

4   For more than a year, I have had a BuzzFeed video: "What Is Female Masculinity?" *BuzzFeed*, August 19, 2015. https://www.buzzfeed.com/karendu/what-is-female -masculinity#.ipP6Zer54.

5   creator of the Mommy A to Z blog, Meredith Hale, wrote: Meredith Hale, "Don't Call My Daughter a Tomboy," *Huffington Post*, November 1, 2016. https:// www.huffpost.com/entry/dont-call-my-daughter-a-tomboy_b_8950530.

6   Catherine Connors wrote a piece on Her Bad Mother: Catherine Connors, "Don't Call Her a Tomboy," *Her Bad Mother*, December 1, 2015. http://herbadmother .com/2015/12/dont-call-her-a-tomboy/.

2

LIVING WITH DEATH

1   Anthony Storr's Feet of Clay, a book about gurus: Anthony Storr, *Feet of Clay: Saints, Sinners, and Madmen—A Study of Gurus* (New York: Free Press, 1996).

2   Jonestown, the Guyana enclave where preacher Jim Jones: The *Casefile True Crime Podcast*, which features true-crime stories from across the globe, covers the story of Jonestown in depth in case 60, which stretches over three one-hour episodes: https://casefilepodcast.com/case-60-jonestown-part-1/.

3   but kept back at least twenty-five kids: The exact number of children kept back
who were fathered by Koresh via polygamous unions with other believers
is unknown, but it was probably at least thirteen. See James Coates, "FBI:
Koresh Wanted His Kids to Perish," Chicago Tribune, April 21, 1993, https://
www.chicagotribune.com/news/ct-xpm-1993-04-21-9304210148-story.html
and Tara Isabella Burton, "The Waco Tragedy, Explained," Vox, April 19, 2018,
https://www.vox.com/2018/4/19/17246732/waco-tragedy-explained-david
-koresh-mount-carmel-branch-davidian-cult-25-year-anniversary.

4   because they believed the apocalypse ... was nonetheless still coming soon: "The
Second Coming of Christ." Seventh-day Adventist Church. https://www
.adventist.org/beliefs/fundamental-beliefs/restoration/the-second-coming
-of-christ/.

5   My first exposure to it wasn't The Simpsons: "The Joy of Sect," The Simpsons,
season 9, episode 14, directed by Steven Dean Moore, written by Steve
O'Donnell (Los Angeles, CA: Fox, February 8, 1998).

6   but I remember watching that, too: See Alasdair Wilkins, "When The Simpsons
Made Fun of That Religion (You Know the One)," A.V. Club, September 27,
2015, https://tv.avclub.com/when-the-simpsons-made-fun-of-that-religion
-you-know-t-1798184997, which says that the DVD's commentary asserts that
the production team of The Simpsons actually tried to "tone down" the simi-
larities between the events that transpired in the Heaven's Gate cult and the
TV episode, which had started to be written before those events took place,
and was in fact originally meant to send up Scientology.

7   Prime Minister Justin Trudeau justified the decision: Josh Wingrove and
Stephanie Flanders, "Trans Mountain Pipeline Was Too Risky for Kinder,
Trudeau Says," Bloomberg News, May 29, 2018. https://www.bloomberg.com/
news/articles/2018-05-29/trans-mountain-pipeline-was-too-risky-for-kinder
-trudeau-says.

8   the worst predictions about Y2K: See Lily Rothman, "Remember Y2K? Here's
How We Prepped for the Non-Disaster," Time, December 31, 2014. https://
time.com/3645828/y2k-look-back/.

9   the doomsday scare: See E.C. Krupp, "The Great 2012 Doomsday Scare," origi-
     nally published in Sky & Telescope Magazine, republished by NASA, November
     9, 2009. https://www.nasa.gov/topics/earth/features/2012-guest.html.

10   In an essay for the New York Times: Dara Horn, "The Men Who Want to Live
     Forever," New York Times, January 25, 2018. https://www.nytimes.com/2018
     /01/25/opinion/sunday/silicon-valley-immortality.html.

11   The guy who popularized buttered coffee in North America: Rachel Monroe, "The
     Bulletproof Coffee Founder Has Spent $1 Million in His Quest to Live to 180,"
     Men's Health, January 23, 2019. https://www.menshealth.com/health/a25902826
     /bulletproof-dave-asprey-biohacking/.

12   the ideology of the inevitability of the death of every individual: George Packer, "No
     Death, No Taxes," New Yorker, November 21, 2011. https://www.newyorker.com
     /magazine/2011/11/28/no-death-no-taxes.

13   something Julia Cooper writes: Julia Cooper, The Last Word: Reviving the Dying
     Art of Eulogy (Toronto: Coach House Books, 2017).

3

ON BEING BIPOLAR

1   half a million workers are out sick with mental health issues weekly: See Carmen
     Chai, "500,000 Canadians Miss Work Each Week Due to Mental Health
     Concerns," Global News, May 5, 2017. https://globalnews.ca/news/3424053
     /500000-canadians-miss-work-each-week-due-to-mental-health-concerns/.

2   sixty percent of people diagnosed bipolar are unemployed: Charles L. Bowden,
     "Bipolar Disorder and Work Loss," American Journal of Managed Care 11
     (2015): S91–S94. https://www.ajmc.com/journals/supplement/2005/2005-06
     -vol11-n3suppl/jun05-2073ps91-s94/.

3   Stephen Fry's 2006 documentary, The Secret Life of the Manic Depressive: Stephen
     Fry: The Secret Life of the Manic Depressive, television broadcast, directed by
     Ross Wilson (London, UK: BBC, 2006).

4   though it affects women at more or less the same rate: See Arianna Diflorio and Ian
     Jones, "Is Sex Important? Gender Differences in Bipolar Disorder," International
     Review of Psychiatry 22, 5 (2010): 437–52. doi: 10.3109/09540261.2010.514601.

5   *twice as likely as people with unipolar depression, to kill themselves:* See, for example, M. Pompili, X. Gonda, G. Serafini, M. Innamorati, L. Sher, M. Amore, Z. Rihmer, and P. Girardi, "Epidemiology of Suicide in Bipolar Disorders: A Systematic Review of the Literature," Bipolar Disorders 15, 5 (2013): 457–90. doi: 10.1111/bdi.12087.

6   *has a gloomier prognosis and stigma:* Esmé Weijun Wang, "Who Gets to Be the 'Good Schizophrenic'?" BuzzFeed, April 7, 2016. https://www.buzzfeednews.com/article/esmewwang/who-gets-to-be-the-good-schizophrenic#.amGglB7dV.

7   *Women with bipolar disorder are at a very high risk:* This information about bipolar disorder and pregnancy is important, but it's about "women," and I'm not a woman ... so in order to keep the quotation within the flow of the essay, I placed it in parentheses rather than dismantling the language.

DENEIGE

1   *Queer theorist Didier Eribon wrote an entire book on insult as the making of the gay self:* Didier Eribon, Insult and the Making of the Gay Self (Durham, NC: Duke University Press, 2004).

4

LIKE A BOY BUT NOT A BOY

1   *when Kim Kardashian was pregnant with North and the entire tabloid press was obsessed with her weight gain:* See Michelle Ruiz, "Why Was America So Mean to Pregnant Kim Kardashian?" Vogue, May 31, 2015. https://www.vogue.com/article/kim-kardashian-pregnant-media-hate.

2   *On Instagram, I followed two different kinds of accounts:* @the_illustrator_of_curves is one, in the first category; in the second, my favourite tomboy style account no longer appears to be active, and I'm currently appreciating the wider diversity of bodies and gender presentations and styles on the #theythem hashtag.

5

DEATH AND BIRTH

1   Maternal mortality rates are relatively low in Canada: See Sarka Lisonkova, Shiliang Liu, Sharon Bartholomew, Robert M. Liston, and K.S. Joseph, for the Maternal Health Study Group of the Canadian Perinatal Surveillance System, "Temporal Trends in Maternal Mortality in Canada II: Estimates Based on Hospitalization Data," Journal of Obstetrics and Gynaecology Canada 33, 10 (2011): 1020–30. https://www.jogc.com/article/S1701-2163(16)35051-4/pdf.

2   a more recent meta-study: Sophie Grigoriadis, Andrew S. Wilton, Paul A. Kurdyak, Anne E. Rhodes, Emily H. VonderPorten, Anthony Levitt, Amy Cheung, and Simone N. Vigod, "Perinatal Suicide in Ontario, Canada: A 15-Year Population-Based Study," Canadian Medical Association Journal 189, 34 (2017): E1085–E1092. doi: 10.1503/cmaj.170088.

3   the opioid crisis killed over 14,700 people: Special Advisory Committee on the Epidemic of Opioid Overdoses, National Report: Opioid-Related Harms in Canada Web-Based Report (Ottawa: Public Health Agency of Canada, December 2019). https://health-infobase.canada.ca/substance-related-harms/opioids.

4   thousands more people would have died: Health Canada, Naloxone: Save a Life Fact Sheet (Ottawa: Government of Canada, March 2019). https://www.canada.ca/en/health-canada/services/publications/healthy-living/naloxone-save-a-life-fact-sheet.html.

5   fifteen years shorter than the average: Canadian Press, "Lifespan of Indigenous People 15 Years Shorter Than That of Other Canadians, Federal Documents Say," CBC News, January 23, 2018. https://www.cbc.ca/news/health/indigenous-people-live-15-years-less-philpott-briefing-1.4500307.

6   a number I can quote without googling: Ose Arheghan, "A Beginner's Guide to Trans Awareness Week," GLAAD, November 14, 2018. https://www.glaad.org/amp/beginner-guide-transweek-2018.

7   In Tom Scocca's article: Tom Scocca, "Your Real Biological Clock Is You're Going to Die," HMM Daily, October 18, 2018. https://hmmdaily.com/2018/10/18/your-real-biological-clock-is-youre-going-to-die/.

8   Presbyterian spiritualist who communed with the dead via mediums and Ouija boards: Blair Fraser, "The Secret Life of Mackenzie King, Spiritualist," Maclean's, December 15, 1951. https://archive.macleans.ca/article/1951/12/15/the -secret-life-of-mackenzie-king-spiritualist.

6

MILK AND TIME

1   I read somewhere that looking at a picture of one's infant: I think the original study may have been D.R. Keith, B.S. Weaver, and R.L. Vogel, "The Effect of Music-Based Listening Interventions on the Volume, Fat Content, and Caloric Content of Breast Milk Produced by Mothers of Premature and Critically Ill Infants," Advances in Neonatal Care 12, 2 (2012): 112–19. doi: 10.1097/ANC.0b013e31824d9842. This study comes up in several articles on how to increase milk production.

2   wrote a feature about dairy farming in Canada: Mirjam Guesgen, "Greener Pastures," Maisonneuve, June 5, 2018. https://maisonneuve.org/article/2018 /06/5/greener-pastures/.

3   Cows are generally fed: See, for example, "What Do Dairy Cows Eat?" Alberta Milk. https://albertamilk.com/ask-dairy-farmer/what-do-dairy-cows-eat/.

4   They drink between 80 and 180 litres: Farm & Food Care Ontario, "Facts & Figures about Canadian Dairy Cows," Milk.org. https://www.milk.org/Corporate /PDF/Students-FarmCare_DairyCows.pdf.

5   Dairy cattle produced over 9.3 billion litres: Agriculture and Agri-Food Canada and Canadian Dairy Commission, "Canada's Dairy Industry at a Glance" (Ottawa: Government of Canada). https://www.dairyinfo.gc.ca/index_e.php ?s1=cdi-ilc&s2=aag-ail.

6   In 2016, a cow from Wisconsin named Gigi: Luke Runyon, "Gigi the Cow Broke the Milk Production Record. Is That Bad for Cows?" NPR.org, March 18, 2016. https://www.npr.org/sections/thesalt/2016/03/18/470938624 /gigi-the-cow-broke-the-milk-production-record-is-that-bad-for-cows.

7   most cows go through three pregnancy and lactation cycles: Wilhelm Knaus, "Dairy Cows Trapped between Performance Demands and Adaptability," Journal of the Science of Food and Agriculture 89, 7 (2009): 1107–14. doi: 10.1002/jsfa.3575.

8   including one from 1990 called "Moosic Is for Cows, Too": A. Evans, "Moosic Is for Cows, Too," Hoard's Dairyman 135 (1990): 721.

9   have shown that slower-tempo music, like Beethoven's Pastoral Symphony: Dr. Anna O'Brien, "Music to My Ears," PetMD, March 1, 2013. https://www .petmd.com/blogs/thedailyvet/aobrien/2013/march/music-influences-milk -production-in-cows-29895.

10   that also happens to score the flying horses segment of Disney's most soporific movie, Fantasia: Ludwig van Beethoven, "Symphony Number 6: Pastoral," Leopold Stokowski & the Philadelphia Orchestra. Fantasia, DVD, directed by James Algar et al., written by Joe Grant et al. (Burbank, CA: Walt Disney Studios, 1940).

11   I come across an article that suggests that not only is breast milk best, but that this milk should ideally come directly from nursing: I didn't save the article, but I'm sure it was part of the news coverage that came out about this Canadian study in Pediatrics: Meghan B. Azad, Lorena Vehling, Deborah Chan, Annika Klopp, Nathan C. Nickel, Jonathan M. McGavock, Allan B. Becker, Piushkumar J. Mandhane, Stuart E. Turvey, Theo J. Moraes, Mark S. Taylor, Diana L. Lefebvre, Malcolm R. Sears, and Padmaja Subbarao, on behalf of the CHILD Study Investigators, "Infant Feeding and Weight Gain: Separating Breast Milk from Breastfeeding and Formula from Food," Pediatrics 142, 4 (2018): e20181092. doi: 10.1542/peds.2018-1092.

12   the first episode of a TV show where a breast milk pump is a prop: "Bare," Workin' Moms, season 1, episode 1, written and directed by Catherine Reitman (Toronto, ON: CBC Television, 2017). https://gem.cbc.ca/media/workin-moms /season-1/episode-1/38e815a-00b70330823.

13   Breastfeeding parents have expressed milk since the 1500s: See Valerie Fildes, Breasts, Bottles and Babies—A History of Infant Feeding (Edinburgh: Edinburgh University Press, 1986), as cited in Kathleen M. Rasmussen and Sheela R. Geraghty, "The Quiet Revolution: Breastfeeding Transformed with the Use of Breast Pumps," American Journal of Public Health 101, 8 (2011): 1356–59. doi: 10.2105/AJPH.2011.300136.

14   when a Swiss company called Medela developed electric pumps: See Megan
     Garber, "A Brief History of Breast Pumps," Atlantic, October 21, 2013. https://
     www.theatlantic.com/technology/archive/2013/10/a-brief-history-of-breast
     -pumps/280728/.

15   given that the average Canadian consumes about sixty-six litres of milk a year:
     Agriculture and Agri-Food Canada and Canadian Dairy Commission,
     "Canada's Dairy Industry at a Glance" (Ottawa: Government of Canada).
     https://www.dairyinfo.gc.ca/index_e.php?s1=cdi-ilc&s2=aag-ail.

16   but they are smaller cows and lower producers, in general: See Jud Heinrichs,
     Coleen M. Jones, and Ken Bailey, "Milk Components: Understanding Milk
     Fat and Protein Variation in Your Dairy Herd," Pennsylvania State University,
     May 5, 2016, https://extension.psu.edu/milk-components-understanding
     -milk-fat-and-protein-variation-in-your-dairy-herd and Caitlin Kasbergen,
     "Comparison of Profitability Jerseys vs. Holsteins, Including Benchmarks
     Comparisons for Production, Reproduction, Health and Costs of Production,"
     California Polytechnic State University, San Luis Obispo, March 2013, https://
     digitalcommons.calpoly.edu/dscisp/75.

17   many large herds of Holsteins will include a couple Jerseys to bump up their milk's fat
     and protein content: See Mike Opperman, "Four Steps to a Higher Fat Test,"
     Dairy Herd Management, May 14, 2019. https://www.dairyherd.com/article
     /four-steps-higher-fat-test.

18   teaching cow at the University of Guelph: the cow once even showed up on the
     Rick Mercer Report, season 3, episode 14 (Toronto, ON: CBC Television, 2006).
     See the clip here: https://youtu.be/jzv_OeVGhlI.

7

ON CLASS AND WRITING

1   Like some Canadian version of Mac McClelland: Mac McClelland, "I Was a
     Warehouse Wage Slave," Mother Jones, March/April 2012. https://www.mother
     jones.com/politics/2012/02/mac-mcclelland-free-online-shipping-warehouses
     -labor/.

2   Jonathan Kay, then editor of the Walrus, published a short piece about class and jour-
    nalism: Jonathan Kay, "Diversity's Final Frontier," Walrus, November 3, 2015.
    https://thewalrus.ca/diversitys-final-frontier/.

3   a stellar rejoinder to his piece: Karen K. Ho, "Meritocracy Is a Lie," Walrus,
    November 4, 2015. https://thewalrus.ca/meritocracy-is-a-lie/.

4   I went on a TVOntario panel: "Too Much Stuff?" The Agenda with Steve Paikin,
    season 8, episode 83 (Toronto, ON: TVOntario, 2013). http://tvo.org/video/
    programs/the-agenda-with-steve-paikin/too-much-stuff. The transcript is
    available here: https://www.tvo.org/transcript/2091107/too-much-stuff.

8

THE BOTTOMLESS PIT OF SELF-LOATHING / A PEAK

1   the rock climbing movie Free Solo: Free Solo, DVD, directed by Elizabeth Chai
    Vasarhelyi and Jimmy Chin (Washington, DC: National Geographic, 2018).

9

WHAT I LEARNED TRUEING BIKE WHEELS

1   There is a tome called the Big Blue Book of Bicycle Repair: My edition is C.
    Calvin Jones, BBB-2: Big Blue Book of Bicycle Repair, 2nd ed. (Saint Paul, MN:
    Park Tool, 2008).

2   move the work area of the bike closer to you: C. Calvin Jones, BBB-2: Big Blue Book
    of Bicycle Repair, 2nd ed. (Saint Paul, MN: Park Tool, 2008), 8.

SORAYA

1   Soraya wrote a piece for Longreads called: Soraya Roberts, "The Queer Generation
    Gap," Longreads, November 23, 2018. https://longreads.com/2018/11/23/the
    -queer-generation-gap/.

10

MOM, DAD, OTHER

1   a piece about non-binary parenthood I co-wrote: The feature, co-written with
    Kim Fu, is called "Beyond Mom 'n' Pop" and was published by Hazlitt on
    September 11, 2015. At the time of writing, the comment can still be found if

you go to the link and scroll down: https://hazlitt.net/feature/beyond-mom -n-pop.

2 *it remains true that for the majority of straight couples with kids*: See Claire Cain Miller, "How Same-Sex Couples Divide Chores, and What It Reveals about Modern Parenting," *New York Times*, May 16, 2018. https://www.nytimes.com /2018/05/16/upshot/same-sex-couples-divide-chores-much-more-evenly -until-they-become-parents.html.

3 *I just want to be as universally revered*: Zoe Whittall (@zoewhittall), Twitter post, May 13, 2015. https://twitter.com/zoewhittall/status/598477320597446656.

4 *Maybe a "Not the mama" iron-on?*: Shirarose, my editor, reminded me that the baby dinosaur from *Dinosaurs*, whose catchphrase was "Not the Mama!" was named Sinclair!

5 *While feminism has tried to move the needle on gendered divisions of labour in parenting*: See, for example, Brigid Schulte, "The Second Shift at 25: A Q&A with Arlie Hochschild," *Washington Post*, August 6, 2014. https://www .washingtonpost.com/blogs/she-the-people/wp/2014/08/06/the-second-shift -at-25-q-a-with-arlie-hochschild.

11

MILK AND GENERATIVENESS

1 *once shared an illustration on Twitter*: Anne Thériault (@anne_theriault), Twitter post, October 9, 2017. https://twitter.com/anne_theriault/status /917456289969639424.

2 *put on a production of The Tale of Peter Rabbit*: I'm not sure if this was an adaptation of *The Tale of Peter Rabbit*, by Beatrix Potter, or simply a one-act production of *The Adventures of Peter Rabbit and His Friends*, a play that was adapted from Potter's books and published by Dramatic Publishing in 1994.

3 *A trans dad, Trevor MacDonald, pitched a column*: The column was published as Trevor MacDonald, "Father, Mother: A Trans Dad's Call to End Gender-Restrictive Parenting," *This Magazine* (January/February 2013): 10–11.

4 *The roles of mothers and fathers are not interchangeable*: MacDonald quotes from the letter in his column, mentioned above; this quote is available via the CBC's coverage of the incident: "Breastfeeding Group Rejects Transgender Dad's

Leadership Bid," CBC News, August 20, 2012. https://www.cbc.ca/news/canada /breastfeeding-group-rejects-transgender-dad-s-leadership-bid-1.1284289.

5   To produce breast milk, mothers literally melt their own body fat: Angela Garbes, "The More I Learn about Breast Milk, the More Amazed I Am," Stranger, August 26, 2015. https://www.thestranger.com/features/feature/2015/08/26/ 22755273/the-more-i-learn-about-breast-milk-the-more-amazed-i-am.

6   I read "breast milk is much more than food": Angela Garbes, "The More I Learn about Breast Milk, the More Amazed I Am," Stranger, August 26, 2015. https://www.thestranger.com/features/feature/2015/08/26/22755273/the-more -i-learn-about-breast-milk-the-more-amazed-i-am.

7   I am buoyed, researching this essay eight years after I edited his column: "Support for Transgender and Non-Binary Parents," La Leche League. https://www.llli .org/breastfeeding-info/transgender-non-binary-parents/.

12

THE PEOPLE'S POETRY

1   Afterwards, he would find himself surrounded by younger poets: See Chris Gudgeon, Out of This World: The Natural History of Milton Acorn (Vancouver: Arsenal Pulp Press, 1996), 88–95; Rosemary Sullivan, Shadow Maker: The Life of Gwendolyn MacEwen (Toronto: HarperCollins, 1995), 101–2.

2   Many of the books that chronicle Acorn and MacEwen's relationship come close: See Chris Gudgeon, Out of This World: The Natural History of Milton Acorn (Vancouver: Arsenal Pulp Press, 1996); Rosemary Sullivan, Shadow Maker: The Life of Gwendolyn MacEwen (Toronto: HarperCollins, 1995); Richard Lemm, Milton Acorn: In Love and Anger (Ottawa: Carlton University Press, 1999).

3   Acorn started off as MacEwen's "poetic mentor": Chris Gudgeon, Out of This World: The Natural History of Milton Acorn (Vancouver: Arsenal Pulp Press, 1996), 94.

4   she'd said no, writing, "Milt, my love": Quoted in Rosemary Sullivan, Shadow Maker: The Life of Gwendolyn MacEwen (Toronto: HarperCollins, 1995), 113.

5   MacEwen, Gudgeon writes, "fed Milt's lopsided vision": Chris Gudgeon, Out of This World: The Natural History of Milton Acorn (Vancouver: Arsenal Pulp Press, 1996), 113.

6   Richard Lemm, is more explicit: "He had a constant companion": Richard Lemm,
     Milton Acorn: In Love and Anger (Ottawa: Carlton University Press, 1999), 122.

7   she was "ambitious" and saw him as "established": Chris Gudgeon, Out of This
     World: The Natural History of Milton Acorn (Vancouver: Arsenal Pulp Press,
     1996), 112.

8   Al Purdy thought "Gwen was with Milton because Milton was 'getting attention'":
     Rosemary Sullivan, Shadow Maker: The Life of Gwendolyn MacEwen (Toronto:
     HarperCollins, 1995), 120.

9   As Sullivan puts it in Shadow Maker, "Almost as soon as she had married":
     Rosemary Sullivan, Shadow Maker: The Life of Gwendolyn MacEwen (Toronto:
     HarperCollins, 1995), 123.

10   Acorn was "deeply conservative" at heart ... and he wanted to see "supper on the
     table every night": Rosemary Sullivan, Shadow Maker: The Life of Gwendolyn
     MacEwen (Toronto: HarperCollins, 1995), 123.

11   he wrote at least one terrible poem about it: The poem is called "Annie's Son."
     It's a biologically inaccurate poem that depicts an almost witch-like woman
     who wears the bones of her aborted fetus as a necklace. It appears in Milton
     Acorn's Against a League of Liars (Toronto: Hawkshead Press, 1960), and
     Richard Lemm praises it as "explosive" in Milton Acorn: In Love and Anger
     (Ottawa: Carlton University Press, 1999), 114.

12   "One letter from that time begins with 'You Dirty Bitch'": Chris Gudgeon, Out
     of This World: The Natural History of Milton Acorn (Vancouver: Arsenal Pulp
     Press, 1996), 113.

13   "accus[es] her of being 'the Great North American Castrator'": Rosemary Sullivan,
     Shadow Maker: The Life of Gwendolyn MacEwen (Toronto: HarperCollins,
     1995), 185.

14   MacEwen wrote back, at least at the beginning: She wrote, for example, "You
     are a great artist, you are not smashed. The injustice I dealt you was not in
     leaving, but in marrying you right off—with an idea of time and permanence
     I actually believed I could deal with. Little I knew of myself, even after what
     you showed me." Quoted in Rosemary Sullivan, Shadow Maker: The Life of
     Gwendolyn MacEwen (Toronto: HarperCollins, 1995), 143.

15   Acorn was still a mess: See Rosemary Sullivan, Shadow Maker: The Life of Gwendolyn MacEwen (Toronto: HarperCollins, 1995), 183; Richard Lemm, Milton Acorn: In Love and Anger (Ottawa: Carlton University Press, 1999), 127; and Chris Gudgeon, Out of This World: The Natural History of Milton Acorn (Vancouver: Arsenal Pulp Press, 1996), 121.

16   Nick Mount writes in his book Arrival: The Story of CanLit, "She was afraid enough of him": Nick Mount, Arrival: The Story of CanLit (Toronto: House of Anansi, 2017), 90.

17   poets Irving Layton and Eli Mandel: Layton was married several times, and his second (ex-)wife wrote a poem to/about him called "Brief to Irving" that is an acerbic takedown of the way Irving used his poetry as a "cudgel" against his wives and ex-wives. See "Brief to Irving," quoted in Joanne Lewis, "Irving's Women: A Feminist Critique of the Love Poems of Irving Layton," Studies in Canadian Literature/Études en littérature canadienne 13, 2 (1988). https://journals.lib.unb.ca/index.php/SCL/article/view/8082.

18   to be raised and "presented to Milton Acorn as the Canadian Poet's Award": Quoted in Chris Gudgeon, Out of This World: The Natural History of Milton Acorn (Vancouver: Arsenal Pulp Press, 1996), 139.

19   Another public plea … reads "Either because of literary politics or a gross ignorance of Canadian poetry": Quoted in Chris Gudgeon, Out of This World: The Natural History of Milton Acorn (Vancouver: Arsenal Pulp Press, 1996), 137.

20   a broad swath of CanLit figures, including Layton, Purdy, and Atwood, showed up at Grossman's Tavern: Nick Mount, Arrival: The Story of CanLit (Toronto: House of Anansi, 2017), 91.

21   Acorn got so drunk he lost his prize cheque twice: Chris Gudgeon, Out of This World: The Natural History of Milton Acorn (Vancouver: Arsenal Pulp Press, 1996), 141–43.

22   had been suspended from UBC pending an investigation into what the university referred to as "serious allegations": Global News Staff, "Acclaimed Author Steven Galloway Temporarily Suspended from UBC Post over 'Serious Allegations,'" Global News, November 18, 2015. https://globalnews.ca/news/2348836/acclaimed-author-steven-galloway-temporarily-suspended-from-ubc-post-over-serious-allegations/.

23   An investigation by a retired Supreme Court Justice, Mary Ellen Boyd, concluded: Canadian Press, "Woman Who Accused UBC Prof, Author Steven Galloway of Sexual Assault Breaks Silence," Vancouver Sun, July 19, 2018. https:// vancouversun.com/news/local-news/woman-who-accused-ubc-prof-author -steven-galloway-of-sexual-assault-breaks-silence.

24   UBC cited "a record of misconduct that resulted in an irreparable breach of the trust placed in faculty members": As quoted in Marsha Lederman, "Author Steven Galloway Fired from UBC after Investigation of 'Serious Allegations,'" Globe and Mail, June 22, 2016. https://www.theglobeandmail .com/news/british-columbia/author-steven-galloway-fired-from-ubc-after -investigation-of-serious-allegations/article30557345/.

25   he received mostly favourable media coverage and was generally depicted as a victim: See, for example, Kerry Gold, "L'Affaire Galloway," Walrus, September 14, 2016, https://thewalrus.ca/laffaire-galloway/ and Gary Mason, "Author Steven Galloway Breaks Silence: 'My Life Is Destroyed,'" Globe and Mail, June 8, 2018, https://www.theglobeandmail.com/arts/books/article-steven -galloway-says-his-life-is-destroyed-after-ubc-payout/.

26   Eventually, it turned out that what many of us suspected—that the slap had been the only substantiated allegation: Marsha Lederman, "Author Steven Galloway Makes First Statement since UBC Firing, Questions Handling of Case," Globe and Mail, November 23, 2016. https://www.theglobeandmail.com/news /national/steven-galloway-ubc-firing/article33004493/.

27   Karen Connelly, an author and Galloway supporter, advanced the gender-swapped "idea for a macabre, best-selling novel": Kaz Connelly, Facebook post, September 18, 2016. https://www.facebook.com/kaz.connelly/posts/10154510643111575.

28   "Forget the novel," wrote Hal Wake: Comment on Kaz Connelly's Facebook post, September 18, 2016. https://www.facebook.com/kaz.connelly/posts /10154510643111575.

29   In November 2016, dozens of Canadian writers signed an open letter, called UBC Accountable: "An Open Letter to UBC: Steven Galloway's Right to Due Process," UBC Accountable, November 14, 2016. http://www.ubcaccountable .com/open-letter/steven-galloway-ubc/.

30   and then, as the story gained traction, a good portion of the putrid swamp of
      online men's rights activists: See Diana Davison, "The UBC Rape Hoax,"
      YouTube, June 23, 2018, https://www.youtube.com/watch?v=pUbFnUlc4QI;
      Brad Cran, "A Literary Inquisition: How Novelist Steven Galloway Was
      Smeared as a Rapist, Even as the Case against Him Collapsed," Quillette, June
      21, 2018, https://quillette.com/2018/06/21/a-literary-inquisition-how-novelist
      -steven-galloway-was-smeared-as-a-rapist-even-as-the-case-against-him
      -collapsed/; and Jonathan Kay, "The Scandal at UBC Keeps Growing—But
      No One Has Been Held Accountable," Quillette, October 17, 2018, https://
      quillette.com/2018/10/17/the-scandal-at-ubc-keeps-growing-but-no-one
      -has-been-held-accountable/.

31   that there should be an "Appropriation prize for best book by an author who
      writes about people who aren't even remotely like her or him": Ashifa Kassam,
      "Canadian Journalists Support 'Appropriation Prize' after Online Furore,"
      Guardian, May 13, 2017. https://www.theguardian.com/world/2017/may/13/
      canadian-journalists-appropriation-prize.

32   several of the nation's most prominent editors ... publicly signed on to establish the
      prize: Ashifa Kassam, "Canadian Journalists Support 'Appropriation Prize'
      after Online Furore," Guardian, May 13, 2017, https://www.theguardian
      .com/world/2017/may/13/canadian-journalists-appropriation-prize; Rachel
      Mendleson, "Jonathan Kay Resigns as Editor of the Walrus amid
      'Appropriation Prize' Backlash," Toronto Star, May 14, 2017, https://www
      .thestar.com/news/gta/2017/05/14/jonathan-kay-resigns-as-editor-of-the
      -walrus-amid-appropriation-prize-backlash.html.

33   In 2018, two more professors: Kate McKenna and Steve Rukavina, "Prominent
      Montreal Writers Investigated in Concordia Sexual Misconduct Allegations
      Inquiry," CBC News, February 18, 2018. https://www.cbc.ca/news/canada/
      Montréal/prominent-Montréal-writers-investigated-in-concordia-sexual
      -misconduct-allegations-inquiry-1.4552716.

34   Coach House Books placed its poetry program on hiatus after one of its poetry board
      members and editors: Scaachi Koul, "A Canadian Poet Who Appeared on a

'Shitty Media Men' List Is Out of His Job," BuzzFeed, January 24, 2018. https://www.buzzfeed.com/scaachikoul/a-canadian-poet-who-appeared-on-a-shitty-media-men-list-is.

35   "for statements the school made during the process that violated his privacy rights and harmed his reputation": As quoted in Terri Theodore, "Steven Galloway Files Lawsuit over Sexual Assault Allegations," HuffPost, October 31, 2018. https://www.huffingtonpost.ca/2018/10/31/steven-galloway-lawsuit_a_23576767/.

36   he subsequently filed a defamation suit against the main complainant in his case: Sarah Berman, "This Canadian Author Is Suing His Sexual Assault Accuser," Vice, November 2, 2018. https://www.vice.com/en_ca/article/a3mwg4/this-canadian-author-is-suing-his-sexual-assault-accuser.

37   it is worth noting that none of the complainants initially received copies of their sections: See Marsha Lederman's reporting, in particular, "Under a Cloud: How UBC's Steven Galloway Affair Has Haunted a Campus and Changed Lives," Globe and Mail, October 18, 2016. https://www.theglobeandmail.com/news/british-columbia/ubc-and-the-steven-galloway-affair/article32562653/.

38   It's further worth noting that at the time he filed suit: See Sarah Berman, "This Canadian Author Is Suing His Sexual Assault Accuser," Vice, November 2, 2018, https://www.vice.com/en_ca/article/a3mwg4/this-canadian-author-is-suing-his-sexual-assault-accuser and Terri Theodore, "Steven Galloway Files Lawsuit over Sexual Assault Allegations," HuffPost, October 31, 2018, https://www.huffingtonpost.ca/2018/10/31/steven-galloway-lawsuit_a_23576767/.

39   who was first wronged by Acorn and then later treated as collateral damage: "I've never been able to swallow the notion that Milton's animosity was because of me getting the award," George Bowering told Chris Gudgeon. "I think he had some strong feelings about Gwen getting it as well. He just didn't feel that he could go after Gwen in public." Quoted in Chris Gudgeon, Out of This World: The Natural History of Milton Acorn (Vancouver: Arsenal Pulp Press, 1996), 138.

40   "[T]he Indian in me is now authenticated": From Milton Acorn (Parkdale, PEI), to Al Purdy (Ameliasburgh, ON), May 8, 1970, as quoted in Al Purdy, Yours, Al: The Collected Letters of Al Purdy, edited by Sam Solecki (Madeira Park, BC: Harbour Publishing, 2004), 158.

41   "You seem to continually mention your Indian ancestry, Milt": From Al Purdy
(Ameliasburgh, ON), to Milton Acorn (Toronto, ON), June 6, 1973, as quoted
in Al Purdy, Yours, Al: The Collected Letters of Al Purdy, edited by Sam Solecki
(Madeira Park, BC: Harbour Publishing, 2004), 227.

42   it was revealed that Galloway had First Nations ancestry: Margaret Atwood
(@MargaretAtwood), Twitter post, November 24, 2016, https://twitter.com/
MargaretAtwood/status/801893807541420036?s=20; Robert Jago, "Why I
Question Joseph Boyden's Ancestry," Canadaland, December 24, 2016, https://
www.canadalandshow.com/question-joseph-boydens-indigenous-ancestry/.

43   Joseph Boyden's own claims to Indigenous heritage: Jorge Barrera, "Author
Joseph Boyden's Shape-Shifting Indigenous Identity," APTN National News,
December 23, 2016. https://aptnnews.ca/2016/12/23/author-joseph-boydens
-shape-shifting-indigenous-identity.

44   elegiac poetry about the coming end of the Indigenous way of life in Canada: See,
for example, the first few lines of Scott's poem "The Onandoga Madonna":
"She stands full-throated and with careless pose, / This woman of a weird
and waning race, / The tragic savage lurking in her face, / Where all her
pagan passion burns and glows." Cited in "'The Onondaga Madonna'"
(1898) by Duncan Campbell Scott and Racialization," CanLit Guides, http://
canlitguides.ca/canlit-guides-editorial-team/poetry-and-racialization/the
-onondaga-madonna-1898-by-duncan-campbell-scott-and-racialization;
originally published in Duncan Campbell Scott, Labour and the Angel
(Boston: Copeland & Day, 1898).

45   Atwood, who compared UBC's investigation process to the Salem witch trials: On
November 16, 2016, Atwood tweeted that "no member of any group is guilty
because accused (as in Salem trials) and no member is not guilty." Margaret
Atwood (@MargaretAtwood), Twitter post, November 16, 2016. https://twitter
.com/MargaretAtwood/status/798902687517511680?s=20). She elaborated on
this in an email to Laura Kane, a Canadian Press reporter, who quoted it in a
November 17, 2016, article: "'Those accused would almost certainly be found
guilty because of the way the rules of evidence were set up, and if you objected
to the proceedings you would be accused yourself,' she wrote. 'Obviously the
university was trying to shield students from something—we are still not

clear as to what, exactly, and if it's a matter of rape then it should be a matter of jail—but their methods appear to have resulted in a big foggy mess.'"
See Laura Kane, "Atwood Compares UBC's Handling of Steven Galloway
Probe to Salem Witch Trials," Toronto Star, November 17, 2016. https://
www.thestar.com/news/canada/2016/11/17/atwood-compares-ubcs-handling
-of-steven-galloway-probe-to-salem-witch-trials.html.

46 *even as, south of the border, the TV adaptation of The Handmaid's Tale: The
Handmaid's Tale,* though often lauded as a feminist text, has just as often
been critiqued by feminists of colour—Black feminists, Indigenous
feminists, Latinx feminists—because it presents common situations in
which women and trans and non-binary people of these backgrounds
have found themselves in via state violence in Canada and the United
States as futuristic horrors. See Angelica Jade Bastién, "In Its First
Season, The Handmaid's Tale's Greatest Failing Is How It Handles Race,"
Vulture, June 14, 2017, https://www.vulture.com/2017/06/the-handmaids
-tale-greatest-failing-is-how-it-handles-race.html and Melanie McFarland,
"Weaponized White Feminism in The Handmaid's Tale and When
They See Us," Salon, June 5, 2019, https://www.salon.com/2019/06/05/
weaponized-white-feminism-in-the-handmaids-tale-and-when-they-see-us/.

47 *Avital Ronell, a feminist philosopher and star comparative literature professor, was
accused of harassment, sexual assault, and stalking:* Colleen Flaherty, "Harassment
and Power," Inside Higher Ed, August 20, 2018. https://www.insidehighered
.com/news/2018/08/20/some-say-particulars-ronell-harassment-case-are-
moot-it-all-comes-down-power.

48 *"We hold that the allegations against her do not constitute actual evidence, but
rather support the view that malicious intention has animated and sustained this
legal nightmare":* Colleen Flaherty's aforementioned "Harassment and Power"
quotes from this letter; this particular quote also appeared in Meghan
Daum, The Problem with Everything: My Journey through the New Culture Wars
(New York: Simon & Schuster, 2019), 107.

49 *"She deserves a fair hearing, one that expresses respect, dignity, and human solicitude in addition to our enduring admiration":* Nell Gluckman, "How a Letter
Defending Avital Ronell Sparked Confusion and Condemnation," Chronicle

of Higher Education, June 12, 2018, https://www.chronicle.com/article/How-a-Letter-Defending-Avital/243650. The letter, in full, is available via file download in a blog post by philosophy professor Brian Leiter, "Blaming the Victim Is Apparently OK When the Accused in a Title IX Proceeding Is a Feminist Literary Theorist," Leiter Reports, June 10, 2018, https://leiterreports.typepad.com/blog/2018/06/blaming-the-victim-is-apparently-ok-when-the-accused-is-a-feminist-literary-theorist.html.

50   the signatories of Galloway's open letter decried his unfair treatment and talked about the Boyd Report on Twitter, implying that they'd seen it: See, for example, this three-tweet thread: "Sexual assault charges have been dismissed by an experienced (female) judge, for what that's worth, after an examination of much evidence." Margaret Atwood (@MargaretAtwood), Twitter post, November 24, 2016, https://twitter.com/MargaretAtwood/status/801910853133963264?s=20; [replying to @MargaretAtwood]: "Have you read the judge's reasons for her findings? If so, can you share them?" Sandy Garossino (@Garossino), Twitter post, November 24, 2016, https://twitter.com/Garossino/status/801915773727846400?s=20; [quote-tweeting @Garossino]: "Hi Sandy. DM me." Margaret Atwood (@MargaretAtwood), Twitter post, November 24, 2016, https://twitter.com/MargaretAtwood/status/801915977344700416?s=20.

51   had more access to platforms like the Globe and Mail: See Gary Mason, "Author Steven Galloway Breaks Silence: 'My Life Is Destroyed,'" Globe and Mail, June 8, 2018, https://www.theglobeandmail.com/arts/books/article-steven-galloway-says-his-life-is-destroyed-after-ubc-payout/; letter from Madeleine Thien to Santa J. Ono, the president and vice-chancellor of UBC, and Gage Averill, dean of Arts, UBC, and Annabel Lyon and Linda Svendsen, acting co-chairs, UBC Creative Writing Program, September 26, 2016, sent by email and published by the Globe and Mail, https://web.archive.org/web/20170425165552/https://www.theglobeandmail.com/static/BC/UBC/thien-letter.pdf; and Marsha Lederman, "Author Brian Brett Heavily Criticizes UBC for Handling of Galloway Case," Globe and Mail, April 3, 2017, https://www.theglobeandmail.com/news/british-columbia/author-brian-brett-heavily-criticizes-ubc-for-handling-of-galloway-case/article34570473/.

52   "When Angela in her short skirt climbed to look at the loft we would sleep in eventually": George Bowering, "The Al Frame," The Al Purdy A-Frame Anthology, edited by Paul Vermeersch, 75–77 (Madeira Park, BC: Harbour Publishing, 2009), 76.

53   Atwood also seemed to reproduce in her writing ... many of the tropes of CanLit as colonial project: See, for example, Alicia Elliott's critique of Margaret Atwood's Survival: A Thematic Guide to Canadian Literature, in Elliott's "Not Your Noble Savage," A Mind Spread Out on the Ground (Toronto: Doubleday, 2019), 151–64.

54   the letters in Yours, Al, that Purdy exchanged with Atwood, Acorn, and Earle Birney: In Al Purdy, Yours, Al: The Collected Letters of Al Purdy, edited by Sam Solecki (Madeira Park, BC: Harbour Publishing, 2004).

55   one who meets God and then must write God's name down in "her little notebook" so as to not forget it: Al Purdy, "Concerning Ms. Atwood," Beyond Remembering: The Collected Poems of Al Purdy, edited by Sam Solecki (Madeira Park, BC: Harbour Publishing, 2000), 496–97.

56   Zachariah Wells's "Citric Bitch's Thinking Is Shit": Zachariah Wells, "Citric Bitch's Thinking Is Shit," Career Limiting Moves, February 7, 2009. http:// zachariahwells.blogspot.com/2009/02/citric-bitchs-thinking-is-shit.html. (Sometime between writing and editing this essay in 2019, the blog was set to private, and the poem is no longer readable there.)

57   she wrote essays about it: See, for example, Margaret Atwood, "MacEwen's Muse," Confrontations, Correspondences, Comparisons, special issue of Canadian Literature 45 (Summer 1970): 24–32. doi: 10.14288/cl.voi45.

58   later, she edited a collection of MacEwen's poetry: Two volumes of Gwendolyn MacEwen's poetry, both edited by Margaret Atwood and Barry Callaghan, were published by Exile Editions in 1993 and 1994. Selected Poetry of Gwendolyn MacEwen, edited and introduced by Atwood, was published by Virago in 1996.

59   When Atwood likened UBC's treatment of Galloway to a witch hunt, it was ironic to the complainants and observers: See Anna Maxymiw, "Occult Favourite," Maisonneuve, Winter 2017, published online January 4, 2018. https:// maisonneuve.org/article/2018/01/4/occult-favourite/.

60   More ironic still is the fact that one of Atwood's most famous poems: Rosemary
     Sullivan, The Red Shoes: Margaret Atwood Starting Out (Toronto: HarperCollins,
     1998), 12.

61   "I think you're a beautiful woman ...": To Margaret Atwood (Toronto, ON) from
     Victoria, BC, January 5, 1987, as quoted in Al Purdy, Yours, Al: The Collected
     Letters of Al Purdy, edited by Sam Solecki (Madeira Park, BC: Harbour
     Publishing, 2004), 433.

62   a statement that asked for "justice" but cited the complainants' allegations as "uncon-
     vincing," "trivial," or "irrelevant": Andreas Schroeder, "Statement by Andreas
     Schroeder," UBC Accountable, November 25, 2016. http://www.ubcaccount
     able.com/signatory-statements/statement-andreas-schroeder/.

13

37 JOBS AND 21 HOUSES

1   They're filming a movie with Sarah Jessica Parker's husband after-hours at camp:
     I think this must have been the made-for-TV movie called The Music
     Man, directed by Jeff Bleckner and starring Matthew Broderick, Kristin
     Chenoweth, and Debra Monk. It aired in 2003 and its filming locations
     are listed on IMDb as Milton, Millbrook, Uxbridge, and Toronto, Ontario
     (https://www.imdb.com/title/tt0293437/). The YMCA day camp was located in
     Lowville Park—technically in Burlington but close to Milton.

2   It takes a thousand years to produce one inch of soil: This line and the accom-
     panying image appear in issue 85 of Adbusters, titled "Thought Control in
     Economics." In that issue, the line reads, "Time it takes to grow one inch of
     soil: 1,000 years." The page is available on a web preview (pages 10–11 of 16):
     https://issuu.com/adbusters/docs/adbusters_85_web_preview.

ACKNOWLEDGMENTS

FOUR ESSAYS IN THIS COLLECTION WERE PUBLISHED PREVIOUSLY. "On Class and Writing" was published as "The Year in Work," with Hazlitt (hazlitt .org); "Tomboy" was published as "The In-Between Space," also with Hazlitt, "Mom, Dad, Other" was published as "I'm a Non-Binary Parent. There Still Isn't Space for Me," with Xtra (dailyxtra.com), and "Like a Boy but Not a Boy" was included in the anthology *Swelling with Pride*, edited by Sara Graefe and published by Caitlin Press.

Thank you to David MacKinnon, the executor of Gwendolyn MacEwen's estate, for permission to reprint lines from "Certain Flowers" at the beginning of "The People's Poetry." I first read this poem in Rosemary Sullivan's biography of Gwendolyn MacEwen, *Shadow Maker*, and it stuck with me.

In researching "The People's Poetry," I interviewed Nick Mount and Hannah McGregor. Although I didn't end up quoting either of them in the piece, our conversations informed and enriched my thinking and knowledge on many of the moments and issues that arise in the piece. Thank you, as well, to friends and colleagues who read an earlier iteration of the essay and gave me vital feedback on it.

When I think about gender and trans history, I think immediately about Morgan M. Page's *One from the Vaults* podcast; basically all of Ivan Coyote's and S. Bear Bergman's books; the writing of Judith Butler, Gwen Benaway, Kai Cheng Thom, and Maggie Nelson; and A.K. Summers's *Pregnant Butch: Nine Long Months Spent in Drag*. Although none of these writers are quoted in this book, I am deeply indebted to and grateful for their work.

The final line of "Mom, Dad, Other" reads, "I need the world to make just enough space for me that I can become completely unremarkable." The only way that I can live my life in a way that even approaches unremarkable (including basic rights, like the option to have the correct gender marker on my ID), is thanks to the trans people and activists who came before me, who made space for themselves and for everyone who came after. Thank you.

The writings of Andrew Solomon, Alicia Elliott, and Esmé Weijun Wang have been indispensable to me as I've thought and written about mental illness and mental health.

When I think about cycling and bike mechanics, I feel the particular need to thank Jobst Brandt, author of The Bicycle Wheel; Paul Fournel, author of Need for the Bike; and my friend and former co-worker and mentor, Emiliano Sepulveda.

The Access Copyright Foundation, via a Marian Hebb Research Grant, and the Canada Council, via a Research and Creation Grant, supported the writing of this book. I'm very grateful for the support. (Relatedly—thank to you to the person who transcribed all of my interviews. You're fastidious and reliable and the only person I would have trusted to transcribe them!)

Thank you to everyone at Arsenal Pulp—Brian, Shirarose, Jaz, Cynara—for your amazing work and for giving this book a home. Thank you, also, to Stephanie Sinclair, who believed in this project before I'd drafted my first book proposal.

A huge thank-you to everyone who spoke with me for "Everyone Is Sober and No One Can Drive": Adam Myatt, April, Ben Rawluk, David

Phillips, Deneige, Erika Thorkelson, Erin Flegg, Jamie, "Jane," John Elizabeth Stintzi, Kai Conradi, Kyle, Laura Friesen, Nadine Boulay, rhean murray, Soraya Roberts. Our conversations were my favourite thing about writing this book.

And thank you to my families: the Bennett-Ha-Kidd-Koks, the Keatses and Osborns, Benny and Emily and Erika and Erin and Beth and Leah. Special thank-yous to Kim, Will, and Sinclair ♥.

andrea bennett is a National Magazine Award–winning writer and editor and the author of one book of poetry (Canoodlers, Nightwood Editions) and two travel guides (Montréal and Québec City, Moon Guides). Like a Boy but Not a Boy is andrea's first book of essays.

andreabennett.ca